THE DEBT COLLECTING MERRY-GO-ROUND

HOW TO DEAL WITH HARASSMENT FROM DEBT COLLECTORS

Anthony Reeves

D1098693

Emerald Publishing
© Anthony Reeves 2011 First Edition
(c) Anthony Reeves 2014 Second Edition

British Cataloguing in Publication data. A catalogue record is
available for this book from the British Library.
ISBN
978-1-84716-463-6

Printed in the United Kingdom by Grosvenor Group London

Cover Photo: Merry-go-Round CCby-SA 2.0 Quinet
Cover Design: Eyeball Media & Publications, Devizes.

THE DEBT COLLECTING MERRY-GO-ROUND

CONTENTS:

Introduction

Introduction

When I began doing debt recovery work in the late 1990s I did not think I would be sitting down a decade later and writing a book about the practices of some debt collectors and large organisations. It is very easy to think - without further consideration - that I have crossed the divide from being an assertive debt collector, once known as Mr Nasty, to a lawyer who has gone soft and is helping people avoid paying what they owe. Such a view is not correct; I have *always* engaged in a "no nonsense" approach to debt collecting and any associated litigation. Perhaps, in the past, I would have been rather more robust in my telephone contact with debtors who had the money but simply refused to pay, but we are living in a different world now and there is greater regulation as to what is acceptable and what is not.

The key difference between my methods, and those adopted by others, is that when I am presented with a genuine dispute, or the individual is not going to pay, I am inclined to consider a method of resolving the dispute; however, if that is not appropriate then court action is likely to be the next step rather than engage in further pressurising contact which might be pointless and has the potential to cross the line into harassment. In the "old days", I always felt that one had a limited opportunity of making a point to a debtor when contact was established. One had to create the necessary impact when making contact (and this I endeavoured to do) but, also, because the opportunity may not arise again as it was unreasonable to repeatedly contact the debtor when there was no genuine reason or no significant change in the situation from when they were last contacted. If I was told that they did not want contact from me then I respected that and realised that the time to make the decision, as to whether or not to issue court action, had come.

As a matter of course, you would attempt direct communication with the debtor but, once you have tried all the various telephone and written techniques to recover the money, and they are refusing to consider Alternative Dispute Resolution -

such as mediation, then court action is an option unless you decide that the debt is not worth pursuing. However, there has been a trend away from following proper procedure, followed by court action, towards continually haranguing a debtor until the coercion succeeds in obtaining payment.

I have no sympathy for a debtor who knows he or she owes the money being claimed and has the means to pay. Neither do I have sympathy for a debtor who wastes the court time in defending a claim on unreasonable grounds. However, where there is a genuine dispute I am against the tactic of using - what can only be described as - harassment to obtain payment. The form of pressure is like a Chinese water torture with that constant drip feed of contact. Once the creditor has sent its entire repertoire of threatening letters and nasty telephone calls, it usually passes the matter to a debt collection company to go through the same cycle. When that fails, often another debt collection company will start the whole process again. This "debt-collecting merry-go-round" spins round and round until either a debtor succumbs to the pressure and pays or takes action to stop it. Those taking action to stop the harassment had often been small in number, perhaps thinking they could not take on the might of the big utility company or bank. This is changing and individuals are realising that they do not have to put up with the bullying. Thankfully, there are still individuals who are prepared to stand up against big business and achieve what is fair and just. Lord Jacob opened his Judgment in Ferguson v. British Gas by stating:

"It is one of the glories of this country that every now and then one of its citizens is prepared to take a stand against the big battalions of government or industry"

This book is not a guide to avoid paying your dues, but hopefully a clear and practical guide to those who are facing the mechanical debt collecting machine of some large organisations; the majority of whom seem to be utility companies and banks. I do not advocate this as being an avenue for people to make a fast buck at the

5

expense of companies whose public profile has not been good in recent years. Instead, it is a guide to what is happening in the real world of debt collecting and what can be done by the ordinary person if caught up in the merry-go-round.

There is an analysis of the various pieces of legislation that has developed to protect the individual from unfair practice. As well as the Guidelines from the new Financial Conduct Authority (FCA), which has taken over the issuing of consumer credit licences to debt collectors from - the now defunct-Office of Fair Trading (OFT), consideration is given to the Protection from Harassment Act 1997 ("PFHA 1997") which, although originally designed to repel stalkers, is now being used to restrain unreasonable intrusion from debt collectors. The important cases such as **Roberts v. Bank of Scotland (2013)** and Ferguson **v British Gas (2009)** are examined and the full text of these Judgments are set out in Appendix 2.

There is practical guidance on what can be done to stop harassment or unfair practice. It is hoped that action taken at an early stage will be sufficient to end the unwanted or unnecessary actions of debt collectors. When it is possible to resolve the matter in other ways they should be pursued first. It is only as a last resort that court action should be contemplated. I do not want to be seen as encouraging people to have a "pop" at banks or utility companies where it is not justified in order to seek compensation. Hopefully by reading the relevant case contained in this book it will be seen that something has to be pretty serious before it can be regarded as harassment.

Since the first edition, there has been the introduction of the provisions in the Tribunal Courts and Enforcement Act 2007 that make changes to bailiff law. However, I intentionally do not consider in great detail the actions of a bailiff; there are some individuals who hold the view that every action taken by a bailiff is illegal and unreasonable. Of course there are some bailiffs who do not behave in the way they should; the so called "bad apples" as there are in every walk of life. The new provisions in the 2007 Act are designed in part to tackle bailiff behaviour.

Some prefer to not pay a small debt or fine so that they can engage in "legal" combat with the bailiff. I often think that in many of these situations, the debtor has had plenty of opportunities to challenge the fine or debt well before the bailiff comes knocking. Also, if an individual is in financial difficulty, there would normally have been the chance to seek debt advice well before the bailiff arrives.

Although the majority of the book looks at unfair practice and harassment, consideration is given to what have driven some organisations to resort to such practices. There is a fair amount of sympathy for creditors in the current climate. It is becoming increasingly difficult to collect debts as the court system is struggling to function effectively through under funding and the court's customer is paying considerably more in court fees for what can be an ineffective method of collecting debts. Little wonder that some have given up on the court system. The ways to reduce the harassment of debtors are explored and the answer seems to be that the courts need to provide an efficient and effective means of recovering money.

Much of the book relies on case studies; I believe that this is an effective way to express legal issues rather than simply set out the relevant law. The reader might be able to identify with the types of scenarios used in these examples. Although they are based on real cases, I should emphasize that none of the case examples are intended to refer to, or comment upon, any real case that may have happened.

Anthony Reeves
September 2014

Chapter 1

What is the Debt-Collecting Merry-Go Round?

There has been a growing tendency in recent years for organisations, especially banks and large utility companies, to subscribe to the "debt-collecting merry-go-round". Businesses will understandably want to recover unpaid debts but the manner of this approach has developed to the extent that in many cases it amounts to harassment and certainly breaches guidance on fair practice.

The classic example of the "debt collecting merry-go-round" is where a creditor will pass an outstanding account to a debt collection company who will go through a sequence of collection stages and, when that fails to recover the debt, the account gets passed to another debt collection company to do exactly the same. The merry-go-round can spin round like this forever unless the harassed individual takes action to stop it.

The debt purchase industry is big business and a major reason for the debt collecting merry-go round. . The price is determined by the 'quality' of the debt. Typical sellers tend to be the banks, building societies, utilities, mail-order companies and car loan businesses; in fact, any organisation that extends credit in large volumes. Before a debt is sold, it will go through the 'in-house' collection process and will usually be referred to debt collection agencies. Eventually, the debt will be written off as "uncollectable" and the debt will be offered for sale. Buyers will then try and use any means to recover the debt in order to make money on the debt purchase

The following case study of **Smith v. UK Energy Plc (UKE)** includes all the typical elements of the debt collecting merry-go-round.

In 2006, Andrew Smith purchased 5 Boundary Close, Newtown. He notified the electricity supplier (UKE) that he was the new occupier. A few weeks later he received an unexpected bill for £2,000 addressed to the occupier of 5 Boundary Avenue, Newtown. Andrew contacted UKE and said this must be a mistake and UKE said yes it was probably intended for a commercial unit that was on the industrial estate a few streets away in Boundary Avenue. Andrew thought nothing more of it and a few months later he received a quarterly bill for £75 and this seemed about right. He paid this bill by bank transfer the following day. However, a few weeks later he received a letter from the credit control department of UKE addressed to A Smith at 5 Boundary Close, Newtown, demanding payment of the £2,100, it had increased from £2,000 as a collection fee of £100 had been added! He contacted UKE and spoke to their credit control call centre, which was probably not based in the UK, and made it clear that this did not relate to him and it was not even his address. Andrew gets further letters from UKE threatening to take him to court within 7 days unless payment was received in full. The following week, Andrew receives a letter from Sledge Hammer Collections (SHC) demanding payment of £2,250 or else court action will follow. Again, a nice little collection charge of £150 had been added. Andrew writes to SHC and copies in UKE explaining the situation and that this does not relate to him. He even mentions that the meter number that is referred to on the bill is not the meter number at Andrew's property! This should surely stop any further contact. The next letter Andrew receives from SHC threatens the attendance of bailiffs and the amount now due has again risen to £2,350. Just when Andrew thought SHC had forgotten about him, he starts receiving telephone calls, initially once a week but their frequency then increases to 4 or 5 per day!

Andrew's recycling bin is getting pretty full from this demand for payment of an account that has nothing to do with him, but it gets even fuller when the following week he gets a letter from Red Letter Collections (RLC) stating that if he does not pay in 7 days court action will commence and the whole sequence of events experienced with SHC starts all over again, culminating in RLC making 4 or 5 telephone calls per day to Andrew.

You may think that the case of UKE and Andrew Smith is a glorified example to make interesting reading. In fact, this is based on an actual case and, if anything, it is less extreme than what actually happened. The cause is a number of factors which include the sheer incompetence of some organisations that have become so large that they do not always know what another part of the business is doing. A lack of experience is another factor as those involved in debt chasing and credit control seem to think that bombarding the customer with letters and telephone calls is all that is required to collect payment.

The debt collecting merry-go-round is a creature born out of a number of factors but the most significant ones contributing to its development are related to the demise of the county courts, including the increasing cost of court fees and the administrative chaos that exists in many courts due a reduction in funding. The civil court process is proving to be an unattractive method of collecting debts especially as the enforcement methods have as much bite as an elderly person with ill-fitting dentures. There is also the prospect of further administrative delays as the courts struggle for adequate resources, especially as mediation seems about to be forced on litigants and government Ministers see this form of ADR as a way to save money in the civil justice system. A pressure to mediate and tame enforcement procedures does not endear large organisations to spend money using a system that, in *their* view, fails to produce results.

"In *their* view" should be emphasized because to judge whether something is effective, or not, it would be fair to assess what you hope to achieve from the current system. The civil court process has never - in recent years - been a particularly robust method for chasing debts. If you are chasing debtors who have the ability to pay and the creditor is prepared to spend the money (and the time) it takes to recover a debt then perhaps the court system is relatively effective. However, if you are trying to recover money relatively quickly and cheaply from those who do not have the means to pay apart from small amounts over a prolonged period of time, you would not view the court system as an effective option. Some large organisations that fuel the debt collecting merry-go-round seem not to be able to understand, or choose to ignore this because the state fails to provide an effective legal system to collect debts It is wrong to ignore the law and resort to harassment, especially where such organisations can afford to use the court system unlike many ordinary people. In a time of economic difficulty, and the need to reduce the budget deficit, if large companies moved away from the courts then this would reduce resources because the current system of making the county courts largely dependent on court fees would mean a fall in revenues and a further drop in the level of service provided.

As mentioned earlier, some organisations have become so large that they do not always know what another part of the business is doing and this is undoubtedly a factor behind this merry-go-round. A lack of experience or training is another factor as those involved in debt chasing and credit control seem to think that bombarding the customer with letters and telephone calls is all that is required to collect payment.

The example of UKE and Andrew Smith is a classic case of a utility company and/or a debt collection company not updating the information they have concerning a particular account. Lawyers are mocked for using the phrase "taking instructions" but everything has to be done on the say-so of the client. One wonders whether many of these debt collection companies actually report back to their clients the crucial and critical information concerning disputes that are raised by those they are chasing. The evidence suggests that, even if they do, they fail to update their records and merely continue with the broken record technique. As an experienced debt litigator, I am surprised by this attitude or sheer incompetence. Surely, if you were to investigate the claims of a customer that the money was not due (and this unearths evidence and documents which support the fact that the customer's version of events is not correct) then you would do so as it puts you in a

11

strong position when it comes to negotiating repayment. Too often, a reply to a customer's query is met by a rather bland and standard reply that does not adequately address the issue.

As well as not taking proper instructions from their clients, I often wonder why some organisations entrust debt collection companies to deal with cases that involve points of contract law about which they clearly do not have the appropriate knowledge or understanding. A typical example is below in the case of **OK Energy UK and Mr Robert Evans.**

Mr Evans runs a restaurant. He took on the lease of the restaurant from his sister Leanne. Leanne had an electricity supply account for the restaurant. When she had the account, she was on a high tariff; when Mr Evans took on the lease of the restaurant he applied to OK Energy UK to take on the electricity supply account. OK Energy agreed to enter into a contract. This was done verbally on the telephone and no terms were pointed out to him before they started supplying him. Mr Evans received bills from OK Energy and for the first 9 months everything seemed fine and he paid the bills which were calculated on their standard tariff of 10 pence per unit. In month 10, Mr Evans decides he wishes to switch to New Source Energy Plc. Then, unexpectedly, Mr Evans receives a recalculated bill using a tariff of 20 pence per unit. Mr Evans contacts OK Energy UK and queries why he has received this new bill for the period for which he has already paid in full. OK Energy state that it is a cancellation fee and was contained in their terms and conditions at the time he took on the supply.

OK Energy needs to understand some basic principles of contract law. For terms to be incorporated into the contract the term must fulfil several requirements. The terms should be given to the other party at the time of entering into the contract or, at least, reasonable steps should have been taken to bring the terms to the attention of the other party. In the case of OK Energy, there were no terms brought to the attention of Mr Evans at the time of entering into the supply agreement about paying a higher rate in the event that he decides to switch suppliers.

As well as the situation of the obvious dispute, such as in the case of the alleged debtor never having received the electricity or any other chargeable service, there are cases of individuals being harassed for money they clearly do not have. It may be said that they are merely hiding their true financial position but it may not come as a surprise that some individuals, possibly vulnerable people who are genuinely without funds, are chased so hard that they either seek money from loan sharks or do worse and contemplate taking their own life. This is not a case of being melodramatic. These situations *do* happen and keep on happening. The following case of **String v. Big UK Bank** is a typical example of a debtor being harassed into paying more than he can afford:

David String lives in a small bedsit in Newtown. He is 57 years old and works a few hours per week sweeping up at the local supermarket. He gets paid the minimum wage and gets assistance with his rent. He has only been living by himself for the past 6 years since his parents passed away. He has learning difficulties and finds it hard to read and write. One of his few pleasures in life is buying CDs from the local music store. He has a bank account with Big UK Bank. David manages to obtain a personal loan from Big UK Bank for £6,000. It is quite surprising because if the Big UK Bank had done its checks into the earnings of David then he would not have been a good bet for the loan. It is not long before David has spent the money and falls behind with the repayment because he gets made redundant from his job and is totally reliant on benefits. David receives letters chasing the unpaid loan and goes to his local Citizens Advice Bureau who help him complete an income and expenditure sheet showing that he can only afford to make payments of £20 per week. He makes this offer to Big Bank who reject the offer and David continues to receive letters and telephone calls on his pay as you go mobile. CAB writes again to the Recovery Manager at Big UK Bank and states that he has not got the funds to pay more than £20 per month. Big UK Bank responds by saying that they acknowledge he has not got funds, but David continues to receive an increased number of telephone calls and letters from not

13

only Big UK Bank's collection department but from Fast Recovery Collections and Debt Collections R Us.

The scenario of David and the Big UK Bank is not exaggerated. Again, this is based on a true situation. What happened next is that David instructed a lawyer to try and stop the continuous telephone calls that were happening 7 or 8 times a day and the endless letters threatening court action. Despite accepting that David had no funds to make any higher repayments, they continued to chase David. A letter was written to the Big UK Bank which was responded to by saying that until he makes an acceptable offer they will continue to chase David. A formal letter of claim was sent to Big UK Bank requesting that all further contact be through his solicitors and that they accept the offer of instalments especially as they had already acknowledged that he had no funds. Despite the letter of claim, letters chasing payment from David continued to be sent by the couple of debt collecting companies instructed by Big UK Bank and from their credit collections department. There were also numerous telephone calls each day, some of them silent. Even after court proceedings were issued, the letters and the telephone calls continued. The situation had got to the stage that an application for an interim injunction was sought to stop the conduct until the matter could be considered at the full trial. Only at this point did the bank's lawyer wake up and offered an undertaking not to make further contact with David and that all future contact be through his lawyers. It is rather ironic that banks think nothing of ignoring a customer's appointed legal representatives; if a firm of solicitors wrote directly to an individual when they knew, or ought to have known, that solicitors were acting for him or her then that would be a serious professional conduct issue.

When analysing the reasons why Big UK Bank acted in this way, one is puzzled as to why they felt it acceptable to continue to bombard David with constant telephone calls and letters after acknowledging he had very little in the way of funds to repay the debt. Perhaps it was a matter of simply one department not communicating with another, or is it rather more sinister and planned? It could be that these large organisations do not expect individuals to stand up to a large business and certainly not expect them to be able to access and engage appropriate legal advice. With the decline in the availability of legal aid and these types of cases not being attractive to many lawyers on a conditional fee basis ("no win no fee"), it is likely that the individual in this predicament will feel that their only choice is to give in to the constant demands and somehow find money to pay. This pressure could lead to the individual trying to obtain the money they do not have from some rather unsavoury characters, such as loan sharks or, in some cases, being forced into committing illegal acts to raise the funds. That may not necessarily be restricted to stealing but may also involve such things as feeling forced into prostitution, or even worse, feeling so stressed that they take their own life.

If banks read between the lines in cases like David Stringer, they would have discovered that he probably had a learning disability and was vulnerable. Perhaps in the old days when the local bank manager knew his local customers and had the authority to make lending decisions, this might never have happened; I know we like to look back at a bygone era with rose tinted spectacles but customer knowledge not only helps the individual but also assists the bank.

It puzzles me when, surely, it would make better sense to target their collection activities on those who are not in hardship and are simply playing the system. I may be accused of not always being academically rigorous and if I was to look at the figures then they would say "of course we target deliberate non-payers". However, the example of David and my many years experience suggest that the practice of harassing *all* types of debtors into paying is not the exception to the norm but appears to be quite commonplace.

Another common feature of the debt collecting merry go round is the constant threat of legal proceedings without actually taking legal action. A classic letter sent by debt collection companies is as follows:

Dear Sir
FINAL DEMAND BEFORE COURT ACTION
Our client: Big Bank Plc
Amount due: £1,000
Late Payment Charges: £40
Total now due: £1,040.00

To prevent legal action from being taken, it is essential that you settle this debt without delay. Payment should be submitted in full within 7 days or legal action will be issued against you. If Judgment is obtained, enforcement of the debt may be sought by one or more of the following procedures:

1. *Warrant of execution by bailiffs*
2. *Application for attachment of earnings order with your present employer*
3. *Application for a charging order on any property you own*

We would emphasize that should Judgment be entered against you this may affect any future credit application you may make elsewhere. We would also draw your attention to the fact that that all legal costs incurred are usually paid by the debtor.

Yours faithfully
One of Many Debt Collectors Ltd

This might be a typical "letter before court action" sent by debt collection companies but it displays a lack of compliance with pre-action protocol which the court rules require the parties to follow before taking legal proceedings. A "letter of claim" of claim should follow the basic principles set out in the Practice Direction that supplements the court rules. The main criticism of the letter is that it does not mention anything about the nature of the debt except to say that a sum of money is owed to Big Bank Plc. There is a section in the guidance on pre-action conduct that says certain information must be provided where the creditor is a business and the debtor an individual. Annex B states:

ANNEX B

Information to be provided in a debt claim where the claimant is a business and the defendant is an individual

1. Where paragraph 7.4 of the Practice Direction applies the claimant should –

(1) provide details of how the money can be paid (for example the method of payment and the address to which it can be sent);

(2) state that the defendant can contact the claimant to discuss possible repayment options, and provide the relevant contact details; and

(3) inform the defendant that free independent advice and assistance can be obtained from organisations including those listed in the table below.

INDEPENDENT ADVICE ORGANISATIONS

Organisation	Address	Telephone Number	e-mail Address
National Debtline	Tricorn House 51-53 Hagley Road Edgbaston Birmingham B16 8TP	FREEPHONE 0808 808 4000	www.nationaldebtline.co.uk
Consumer Credit Counselling Service (CCCS)		FREEPHONE 0800 138 1111	www.cccs.co.uk
Citizens Advice	Check your local Yellow Pages or Thomson local directory for address and telephone numbers		www.citizensadvice.org.uk
Community Legal Advice (formerly Community		0845 345 4345	www.clsdirect.org.uk

2. The information set out in paragraph 1 of this Annex may be provided at any time between the claimant first intimating the possibility of court proceedings and the claimant's letter before claim.

3. Where the defendant is unable to provide a full response within the time specified in the letter before claim because the defendant intends to seek debt advice then the written acknowledgment should state –

(1) that the defendant is seeking debt advice;

(2) who the defendant is seeking advice from; and

(3) when the defendant expects to have received that advice and be in a position to provide a full response.

4. A claimant should allow a reasonable period of time of up to 14 days for a defendant to obtain debt advice.

5. But the claimant need not allow the defendant time to seek debt advice if the claimant knows that –

(1) the defendant has already received relevant debt advice and the defendant's circumstances have not significantly changed; or

(2) the defendant has previously asked for time to seek debt advice but has not done so.

Back to top

Even if we excuse the letter for not strictly complying with protocol, what will usually happen - and cannot be excused - is that the debt collection agency will probably send such a letter threatening legal action on many subsequent occasions and you start to wonder if legal action will ever start. It becomes a bit like a "Phoney War".[1] In cases where the debtor believes he has an arguable case, it is reasonable, after having explained to the creditor why the debt is disputed, to sit back and see if court action is commenced. Clearly, it is unreasonable conduct where a defendant knows the debt is due and can afford to pay it but waits until court action is actually taken before attempting to defend the debt claim. In these cases, they should face severe cost penalties from the courts. However, I feel that many debt-collecting companies do not address the real issues that arise and cast doubt on whether a debt is actually due. Instead, they will continue the broken record technique of responding to queries by sending a further letter threatening legal action, which in most cases are pretty standard.

---

[1] Phoney War' was the name given to the period of time in World War Two from September 1939 to April 1940 when after the invasion of Poland, people in Britain were waiting for a major attack from Germany.

An alternative to the sending of several rather badly written "letters before court action" is to issue a statutory demand in the hope that the threat of bankruptcy will encourage the reluctant debtor to make payment. Debt collection companies see a statutory demand as a sort of "nuclear" weapon. It is seen as the ultimate device that cannot and will not be resisted by the debtor. An example of a statutory demand is shown at the end of this chapter. Where there is clearly no dispute about the debt being due, it is perfectly reasonable to use a statutory demand but it is often used under the wrong circumstances. There was a time when bankruptcy would have been regarded as a stigma and had serious consequences for certain individuals, such as those involved in public office, but that is perhaps not the case so much these days with the easing of the sanctions for bankruptcy which in turn has led to more people declaring themselves bankrupt. However, the mistake that is made is to issue a statutory demand in situations where there is a dispute.

A debtor has grounds to apply to set aside a statutory demand where the debt is disputed on grounds that appear to the court to be substantial. The meaning of substantial dispute has been the source of some debate. It was thought that the test of what is a substantial dispute was slightly lower than that applied in applications for summary judgment, namely "is there a real prospect of successfully defending the claim". However, recent cases suggest that there is no material difference between the two tests. This point was made in the Court of Appeal case of **Collier v P&MJ Wright (Holdings) Ltd (2008).** The Judgment of Lady Justice Arden is very helpful in explaining what is meant by a substantial dispute.

> "In my judgment, the requirements of substantiality or (if different) genuineness would not be met simply by showing that the dispute is arguable. There has to be something to suggest that the assertion is sustainable. The best evidence would be incontrovertible evidence to support the applicant's case, but this is rarely available. It would in

19

general be enough if there were some evidence to support the applicant's version of the facts, such as a witness statement or a document, although it would be open to the court to reject that evidence if it was inherently implausible or if it was contradicted, or was not supported, by contemporaneous documentation ...There is in the result no material difference on disputed factual issues between real prospect of success and a genuine issue worthy of trial."

The key point from this extract is that, to show a substantial dispute, it has to be more than simply "arguable". There has to be some evidence to suggest or support that, when someone claims there is a dispute, such a claim is sustainable.

Before making the application to the court, you should write to the creditor setting out why you have grounds to set aside the Statutory Demand and invite the creditor to withdraw it. The case of **Frank Heckler and Distance Tutors Ltd** illustrates what should be done where there are grounds to set aside a statutory demand.

Frank Heckler signed up for a distance learning course in information technology. Before he signs the paperwork, he is told by Distance Tutors Ltd that the course is accredited by Microsoft, there will be 10 hours per month of on line tutor assistance and Jason will be able to sit the end of course examination at a college within 50 miles of his home. These issues were important to Frank and without the Microsoft accreditation and being able to take the exam at a local college, he would not have signed up for the course. Frank starts the course and the material provided seems poor. As the course progresses, he discovers that he is not receiving access to the 10 hours per month. He also discovers that the nearest examination centre is 100 miles away. The course fees of £3,000 are payable quarterly and Frank has made the first 2 payments leaving the sum of

£1,500 due. He refuses to pay the remainder and eventually receives a Statutory Demand from Distance Tutors.

Frank refuses to pay the remainder as he believes he was misled about certain key aspects of the course. He points to the fact that when he wrote to Distance Tutors for course information he stated that he wanted a Microsoft recognised course as he wanted to go on and take a more advanced course that required passing a basic IT course which was Microsoft accredited. The literature he received advertising the course had the Microsoft logo on it. Frank writes to Distance Tutors as follows:

> *Dear Sirs,*
> **RE: Information Technology Course**
> *I am in receipt of your Statutory Demand dated the xx/xx/xxxx.*
>
> *I dispute that I owe Distance Tutors the sum of £1,500.I have grounds to set aside this demand under Rule 6.5(4) of the Insolvency Rules 1986 as there is a substantial dispute. The nature of the dispute is set out below.*
>
> *Before signing up for this course I made it clear that I wanted this course to be Microsoft accredited. I refer to a copy of my letter I sent to Distance Tutors prior to enrolling. The course material I received from Distance Tutors contained the Microsoft logo. I have since discovered that Microsoft do not recognise this course.*
>
> *I also made it clear to the representative who visited me to sign me up that I needed to be able to sit the end of course examination at a college within 50 miles of my home in Bristol. I was assured that this was the case. I since discovered that the nearest examination venue is Newcastle which is considerably more than 50 miles away.*

The course brochure I was given stated that I would have on-line access to a tutor for at least 10 hours per month. I was only able to contact my tutor on one occasion in 4 months despite repeated e-mails to him that I needed assistance. I refer to 3 e-mails I sent to my tutor.

I therefore believe that there were misrepresentations on the part of Distance Tutors. The representations that it was Microsoft accredited and that I could sit the examination at a college within 50 miles were both untrue and induced me to sign up for the course. Further, there has been a breach of contract in that I have not been provided with the online tutor time that I was promised at the start of the course.

I invite you to withdraw this statutory demand. If I do not receive confirmation within 7 days that you have withdrawn it, I will make an application to the court to set it aside and will be claiming the costs of doing so.

Yours faithfully
Frank Heckler

To set aside a statutory demand, the following needs to be filed at the appropriate court:

- Application to set aside
- Witness statement in Support

The fact that statutory demands continue to be issued in cases where there are disputes would indicate that some debt collection companies use such tactics to pressurise people into paying what may not actually be due. In view of the increased cost of issuing bankruptcy proceedings, it is also likely that many demands are issued with no real intention of following through with an actual bankruptcy petition. The issuing of statutory demands, with no real intentions of presenting bankruptcy petitions, is grounds for taking action against consumer credit licence holders and action has indeed been taken in such instances, thus incurring large fines being issued by the OFT/FCA.

SUMMARY

The "debt collecting merry-go-round" is a term that describes the process by which some large organisations chase debt, especially consumer debt. It invariably involves endless cycles of letters and telephone calls which - in all honesty - can only be designed to, sometimes, unjustifiably force debtors into paying something to get the collectors off their backs. This bombardment of contact is contrary to taking the next *legitimate* step in the collection process where settlement cannot be reached or there is a genuine dispute (i.e court action or some form of adjudication of the dispute). As will be discussed later, the main reason for the refusal to use court action is that the civil justice system is being neglected in terms of funding and creditors do not see it as being effective.

Chapter 2

What Laws Can Assist The Harassed Debtor?

The previous chapter described what is regarded as the debt collecting merry-go-round. Those caught up in this vicious cycle will want to know what legal measures are available to assist. The law is a combination of statutes and codes of conduct. The most important areas of law include:

1. The Protection from Harassment Act 1997
2. Section 40 of the Administration of Justice Act 1970
3. Regulatory Guidelines: The Financial Conduct Authority (FCA) now controls the issuing of consumer credit licences; until April 2014 it was the Office of Fair Trading. The FCA is developing a new code of conduct but many of the principles carry across the OFT debt collection guidelines.

This book focuses, to a large extent, on the Protection from Harassment Act 1997 because it provides a civil remedy to the harassed debtor. Whilst section 40 of the Administration of Justice Act 1970 makes it a criminal offence to harass a debtor, it should be said that, in order to enforce a breach of this section, would necessitate trading standards or the police bringing a prosecution. The reality is that trading standards departments and the police are overstretched and under resourced; so, unless the matter is very serious, it is unlikely that they would bring a prosecution.

Section 40 of the Administration of Justice Act 1970

Although section 40 does provide a civil remedy, it is worth looking at the wording as to what constitutes an offence of harassment:

"(1) A person commits an offence if, with the object of coercing another person to pay money claimed from the other as a debt due under a contract, he—

(a) harasses the other with demands for payment which, in respect of their frequency or the manner or occasion of making any such demand, or of any threat or publicity by which any demand is accompanied, are calculated to subject him or members of his family or household to alarm, distress or humiliation;

(b) falsely represents, in relation to the money claimed, that criminal proceedings lie for failure to pay it;

(c) falsely represents himself to be authorised in some official capacity to claim or enforce payment; or

(d) utters a document falsely represented by him to have some official character or purporting to have some official character which he knows it has not."

Subsection (1) (a) is important as it describes it as an offence to harass the other with demands which, by their frequency, are calculated to cause distress or humiliation. This would, obviously, apply to situations where the debt collector deliberately makes very frequent contact demanding payment and the frequency of such contact is designed to cause distress and humiliation that makes the debtor pay up.

Subsection (1) (d) would cover a tactic that is often used by debt collection companies and credit control department whereby they complete a Claim Form and send it to the debtor. The debtor may mistakenly believe that the Claim Form has been issued by the Court and so could breach (1) (d) in that it may falsely represent an official court document when the debt collector knows it does not. I have never really understood this tactic. Firstly, the receiving of the real thing from the court is going to have greater impact and so by employing the above tactic prior to raising a *legitimate* court claim, the debtor may not take it seriously. It may be that this tactic continues because of recent increases in court fees which means that debt collectors/credit control departments will try other

25

methods before taking court action even if they are not all permissible by law.

Regulatory Guidelines

Until April 2014, the OFT was charged with the responsibility for issuing consumer credit licences. This regulatory function has been taken over by the FCA who issue these licences for "regulated activity". In certain situations, debt collecting is a regulated activity. The definition of "debt collecting" for the purposes of needing a consumer credit licence is contained in Article 39F of the Regulated Activities Order[2] as amended by The Financial Services and Markets Act 2000 (Regulated Activities) (Amendment) (No.2) Order 2013:

39F.

(1) Taking steps to procure the payment of a debt due under a credit agreement or a relevant article 36H agreement is a specified kind of activity.

(2) Taking steps to procure the payment of a debt due under a consumer hire agreement is a specified kind of activity.

(3) Paragraph (1) does not apply in so far as the activity is an activity of the kind specified by article 36H (operating an electronic system in relation to lending).

(4) In this article, "relevant article 36H agreement" means an article 36H agreement (within the meaning of article 36H) which has been entered into with the facilitation of an authorised person with permission to carry on a regulated activity of the kind specified by that article.

---

[2] Financial Services and Markets Act 2000 (Regulated Activities) Order 2001.

So in essence, a consumer credit licence is required for the taking of steps to recover a debt under a credit agreement or a consumer hire agreement. The meaning of a "credit agreement" is:

...an agreement between an individual or relevant recipient of credit ("A") and any other person ("B") under which B provides A with credit of any amount...

The FCA is developing guidelines for debt collectors who hold consumer credit licences. These guidelines adopt the semblance previously conveyed within OFT debt collecting guidelines. The FCA has produced a specialist sourcebook for credit-related regulated activities (Consumer Credit sourcebook "CONC"). CONC 7 deals with arrears, default and recovery (including repossessions)[3].

Some of the guidelines relevant to debt collection include:

7.3 - treatment of customers in default or arrears (including repossessions): lenders, owners and debt collectors:

[The following is a selection of the requirements]

- a firm[4] must treat its customers fairly
- where customers are in default or arrears, a firm should allow the customer reasonable time and opportunity to repay the debt
- a firm should not develop a policy of refusing to negotiate with a customer who is developing a repayment plan
- a firm must suspend the active pursuit of recovery of a debt from a customer for a reasonable period of time where the customer informs the firm that a debt counsellor is developing a repayment plan

---

[3] http://fshandbook.info/FS/html/FCA/CONC/7

[4] An authorised person

- a firm must not take disproportionate action against a consumer

7.5 - pursuing and recovering payments

[The following is a selection of the requirements]

- a firm must not pursue an individual whom the firm knows or believes might not be the borrower
- a firm must not ignore or disregard a customer's claim that a debt has been settled or is disputed and must not continue to make demands for payment without providing clear justification and/or evidence as to why the customer's claim is not valid.

7.9 - Contact with customers

[The following is a selection of the requirements]

- a firm must not contact customers at unreasonable times and pay due regard to the reasonable requests of customers in respect of when, where and how they may be contacted
- a firm must not unfairly disclose or threaten to disclose information relating to the customer's debt to a third party
- a firm must not act in a way likely to be publicly embarrassing to the customer
- a firm must take reasonable steps to ensure that third parties do not become aware that the customer is being pursued in respect of a debt.

Debt collection visits:

- A firm must ensure that all person's visiting a customer's property on its behalf do not:

    - act in a threatening manner

- enter a customer's property without the customer's consent or an appropriate court order
- refuse to leave a customer's property when reasonably asked to do so

If a consumer credit licence holder seriously breaches the terms of their licence or there are a number of complaints, the FCA has powers to take action and the debt collector would be in danger of losing their licence. The threat of a big fine or losing their consumer credit licence, may be sufficient to make the debt collector stop the course of conduct that amounts to harassment

The Protection From Harassment Act 1997

The Protection from Harassment Act 1997 ("PFHA 1997") was passed following concern about the problem of stalking. It was considered that existing civil and criminal law did not deal with the problem of stalking appropriately and new legislation was therefore required. It is often referred to in the media as 'The Stalking Law'. Recently, there have been further amendments to the Act which specifically refer to the offence of stalking.[5] The PFHA 1997 creates two criminal offences and allows civil courts to make injunctions and award damages.

Section 1 of the PFHA 1997 states that a person must not pursue a course of conduct which amounts to harassment and which he knows or ought to know amounts to harassment of the other. The person whose course of conduct is in question ought to know that it amounts to harassment of another if a reasonable person in possession of the same information would think the course of conduct amounted to harassment of the other. The type of conduct which amounts to harassment depends on the circumstances but the Act states that causing alarm or distress is

---

[5] Section 111 of The Protection of Freedoms Act 2012

conduct that can amount to harassment.[6] A course of conduct means at least two incidents. Although two can be sufficient, if the incidents occur during an extended period of time then a court might not regard each incident as being part of a course of conduct. There have been several cases on what constitutes harassment in civil cases in recent years although there have not been many reported cases involving debt collectors. The courts are keen to emphasize that individuals must expect to put up with a certain amount of inconvenience. The difficulty is where does it cross the line from inconvenience to harassment?

It has been argued that the PFHA 1997 is badly drafted and that the definition is rather vague. On the hand, others have praised the flexibility of the Act and this has given rise to it being used in a variety of situations including being an effective weapon against nuisance creditors.

Ferguson v British Gas

There have been cases on how grave the course of conduct had to be before it could be regarded as harassment but the case of **Ferguson v British Gas (2009)[7]** was important because of its comments in relation to debt collecting activities. In this case, Ms Ferguson used to be a customer of British Gas until around May 2006. From August 2006 to January of the following year, British Gas sent Ms Ferguson bill after bill and threatening letter after threatening letter. Nothing she did stopped it. The letters contained threats to cut off her gas supply, to start legal proceedings and (of particular concern to Ms Ferguson being a business woman) a threat to report her to credit references agencies. Ms Ferguson wrote many letters and mainly received no response. Sometimes

---

[6] Section 7(2) of the Protection From Harassment Act 1997

[7] [2009] EWCA Civ 46, - full judgment in Appendix 2

she received apologies and assurances that the matter would be deal with, but then the bills and threats continued. Even when her solicitor wrote on her behalf, no reply was received. Ms Ferguson issued court proceedings claiming harassment under the PFHA 1997. British Gas made an application strike out the claim before a trial, as they claimed that it showed no reasonable ground for bringing the claim. The application to strike was refused and so British Gas sought and obtained permission to appeal the decision to not strike out the claim.

The Court of Appeal had to consider whether the case should be struck out, or that there were reasonable grounds for bringing the claim and, thus should be allowed to proceed to a trial. British Gas had claimed that the conduct was not serious enough to be harassment and that the letters were computer-generated so, therefore, could not be construed as harassment. The Court of Appeal held that it was, at the very least, strongly arguable that British Gas' conduct was of sufficient gravity to constitute harassment under the Protection from Harassment Act 1997 and the matter should be allowed to proceed to trial.

British Gas accepted that its actions towards Ms Ferguson amounted to a "course of conduct". However, they claimed that the conduct was not sufficient to amount to harassment - that is both a civil wrong (*section 3(1)*) and a crime (*section 2(1)*). According to British Gas, Parliament could not have intended that merely annoying or aggravating matters of everyday life would be criminalised. The Court of Appeal rejected this contention. The case law made it clear that all sorts of conduct could amount to harassment and that the context in which the conduct occurred was also relevant. Jacob LJ said that he accepted that a course of conduct must be grave before the offence or tort of harassment existed, but that he was unable to conclude that British Gas's conduct could not satisfy the test. On the contrary, he believed that at the very least, it was strongly arguable that they did. He thought a jury or magistrate could reasonably conclude that the persistent and continued conduct was on the wrong side of the "line", thus amounting to oppressive and unacceptable conduct.

British Gas argued two further points relating to the gravity of the alleged conduct. First, they attempted to downgrade the serious nature of their threats, by arguing that Ms Ferguson could not have been very distressed by the letters since she knew the threats were not justified. Jacob LJ rejected this ("absurd") argument. The other argument was that, as the correspondence was computer-generated, it should not have been taken as seriously as if it had come from an individual. This argument received short thrift. Jacob LJ said that British Gas programmed the information that went into the computers and they were responsible for what had happened. It did not matter if the correspondence was of a standard nature generated by computers. As Lord Justice Sedley stated:

"One excuse which has formed part of British Gas's legal argument for striking out the claim, and which has been advanced as incontestable and decisive, is that a large corporation such as British Gas cannot be legally responsible for mistakes made either by its computerised debt recovery system or by the personnel responsible for programming and operating it. The short answer is that it can be, for reasons explained by Lord Justice Jacob. It would be remarkable if it could not: it would mean that the privilege of incorporation not only shielded its shareholders and directors from personal liability for its debts but protected the company itself from legal liabilities which a natural person cannot evade. That is not what legal personality means".

So British Gas lost their Appeal over the refusal to strike out the claim. However, the claim did not proceed to a trial as an out of court settlement was reached. Although the matter did not go to trial the Judgment of the Court of Appeal dismissing the interim application of British Gas was of importance because it opened the door to the fact that suppliers and debt collection companies who pursue the wrong person or pursue a person after a bill has been settled may risk both civil and criminal liability. In addition, it highlighted the fact that suppliers may not be able to avoid responsibility for correspondence with consumers on the grounds that these letters were computer-generated.

Roberts v Bank of Scotland

The Court of Appeal decision in **Roberts v Bank of Scotland (2013)**[8] provides a very useful commentary as to when the course of conduct crosses the line and becomes harassment in the context of debt collection. The facts of the case were that Miss Roberts had an account with Halifax and, during 2007 and 2008, she held a current account, credit card account and a loan account. There were periods where she exceeded her overdraft limit. With a view to resolving the issues, the bank decided to contact Miss Roberts by telephone. According to the bank's log, at least 547 calls or attempted calls were made to Miss Roberts over the period from December 2007 to January 2009. The vast majority of the calls were made in the first half of 2008. She made it very clear to the bank that she did not want to talk to them and she wanted them to stop telephoning. The bank staff refused to stop and insisted that they would continuing telephoninguntil Miss Roberts would answer her security questions and discussed her financial position. She became distressed by the bombardment of the telephone calls from the bank and regarded it as harassment.

Miss Roberts recorded some of the calls and the transcripts were produced at the trial. The following extract contained in the Judgment makes remarkable reading:

"AR	Why am I getting these calls when I keep asking you to stop ringing me?
Caller	Is this Amanda I'm talking to, yeah?
AR	Are you deaf?

---

[8] [2013] EWCA Civ 882 - full judgment in Appendix 1

Caller	Right, Amanda we won't stop the calls unless we talk to you
AR	And do you know that I keep asking over and over again for you to not ring me? And I will contact my bank directly and speak to them
Caller	Right
AR	Over and over again I keep asking you and you keep ringing me, I'm getting calls at ten past eight in the morning and ten to ten at night
Caller	You will do
AR	I will do? Over and over again?
Caller	Yes, do you want me to stop the calls coming out to you?
AR	Excuse me! How many times have I asked?
Caller	Right, so we need to have a quick chat then, OK? I just need....
AR	No I don't think so! Stop ringing me!
Caller	OK, we'll give you a ring later
AR	No you won't!
Caller	Yes we will!
AR	Oh, and you're just going to keep doing it over and over again?
Caller	Yes, until you talk to us, OK?

AR	And that's how you behave as a business is it?
Caller	What? Because we want to talk?
AR	You call it talking? I call it harassment!

Lord Justice Jackson in his Judgment in **Roberts** went through the various authorities on what constitutes harassment. He started his analysis by saying:

"In their daily lives most people regularly interact with friends, colleagues, opponents, acquaintances and strangers. Inevitably not all of these interactions are harmonious"

He referred to the case of **Ferguson v British Gas (2009).** In **Ferguson,** Lord Justice Jacob commented that:

> *18. ....What makes the wrong of harassment different and special is because, as Lord Nicholls and Lady Hale recognised, in life one has to put up with a certain amount of annoyance: things have got to be fairly severe before the law, civil or criminal, will intervene.*

In the case of **Roberts v Bank of Scotland,** what made the conduct severe was the sheer volumes of calls and the content of those calls. As Lord Jackson remarked that Miss Roberts had made it abundantly clear that she did not wish to receive calls from the bank and said she was perfectly entitled to adopt that position. So, after the bank had called a few times and received the same response, it should have been obvious that it would achieve nothing and, thereafter, there was no possible justification for continuing to call Miss Roberts.

The comments of Lord Jackson are significant because the lower courts sometimes take a less favourable view if you decide that you do not wish to communicate further with the creditor/debt collector. An example of this was in the case of **Cox v British Gas Trading (2013)** heard in July 2013 at Slough County Court.[9] The case concerned a claim by Mr Cox for harassment against British Gas. Mr Cox claimed he had been harassed by British Gas who claimed he owed money for energy charges at a property in Dean Street where his business had once occupied. Mr Cox claimed that they left the premises and the landlord had allowed others into occupation of the property and so ending his lease. Mr Cox supplied substantial information to British Gas but they continued to pursue him for the charges as they received the lease from Landlord which showed him as being responsible for the charges. District Judge Devlin heard the case and at paragraph 7 of his Judgment he said:

"The first question to establish is whether the conduct constitutes harassment, and I am satisfied that it does not constitute harassment. The claimant has unrealistically expected the defendant to investigate the title, the validity of the lease, to look at the Land Registry, but the Defendants had a lease which was provided to them which showed that the claimant was a lessee of the premises in question in Dean Street, and at that point the onus was on the claimant to show that he was not responsible for the supply. He wrote three emails, the court has looked at them, in November and December 2010, saying that he was not liable, but he does not give any detail, no detailed information or any positive case about why it was that he was not responsible for the supply. Only on 5th April 2011 did he appear to have set out a more detailed account, and that was by email to Theresa Mason, in which he refers to the lease having been forced upon them under duress, misrepresentations and illegal action by the landlord at that time. He talks about an ongoing case between "us", meaning himself and Mr Gilbert and the landlord. He talks

---

[9] The author was involved in this case.

about the locks being changed and no further access to the premises. But it would have been open to him to supply much more detail and documentation or leads about all those points. He refers to the dispute between him and the landlord, but that is not a matter for British Gas and it is unrealistic to expect that British Gas could carry out all those investigations. He could have provided documents about his ongoing case in relation to the police, or showed that he had no control over the building. He refused to speak to representatives of British Gas on the phone. The court found that his explanation for that was not at all convincing, in that he had been told by a debt advisor, not to put things in writing. But he could have had his own log of what was said to British Gas and they would have recorded their own log of what had been said by him to them. That was the obvious thing to do; to call them and tell them, to speak to them on the phone about the situation."

The Judge took the view that Mr Cox could have supplied more information to British Gas. However, Mr Cox had sent 12 emails regarding the dispute prior to him bringing a claim in harassment, but Mr Cox believed that British Gas had either ignored or not provided a substantive response to 9 of them. The judge refers in the extract to an email in April which he credits as being a full account. However, he does not mention that British Gas did not appear to respond or react to the content. So, in Mr Cox's view, he had supplied substantial information before he decided not to speak to British Gas on the telephone.

However, despite the contrary view in some lower courts, it is arguable that if you have supplied sufficient information as to why you dispute the debt and do not wish to receive further calls, then as Lord Jackson said in **Roberts** you are entitled to take that position.

The courts understandably expect conduct complaints to be fairly severe as they do not want the "floodgates" to open. However, to a certain extent, you have to take the "claimant as you find him", as per the old egg shell principle. The courts, in recent cases, have paid particular importance to "the little person taking on the big organisation". As Lord Justice Jacob said in **Ferguson v British Gas:**

> *"It is one of the glories of this country that every now and then one of its citizens is prepared to take a stand against the big battalions of government or industry. Such a person is Lisa Ferguson, the claimant in this case. Because she funds the claim out of her personal resources, she does so at considerable risk: were she ultimately to lose, she would probably have to pay British Gas's considerable costs."*

The context in which the course of conduct is occurring is very relevant as to whether or not it has crossed the line into harassment. Conduct which may begin with what is a legitimate inquiry may become harassment within the meaning of section 1 of the 1997 Act by reason of the manner of it being pursued and its persistence. In a "debtor-creditor" scenario, this is a relationship which is often unbalanced in favour of the creditor. The contacting of the debtor by the creditor in relation to paying an unpaid debt may well be a legitimate inquiry but it can become harassment by the manner it is pursued and or its persistence. So if the debtor has responded to the contact by setting out a legitimate reason for disputing the debt, then simply repeating the request for payment will probably cross the line into harassment. Another example of context might be where the creditor persists with contacting the debtor after him/her making it clear that they want contact to be via their appointed representative, such as their solicitor. Another example of the importance of the context might be where the creditor becomes aware of the debtor's vulnerability, for example the debtor has learning difficulties or mental health issues, but persists with the demands for payment while ignoring the requirement to exercise greater sensitivity.

A corporation cannot make a claim under section 3 of the PHA. If there is a course of conduct against a company that involves harassment of individuals who are employees, directors or shareholders of the company, each of those individuals may take action. However, in such cases it is usual for a director/employee to sue as a representative of all employees of the company.

SUMMARY

Harassment includes a course of conduct that the perpetrator knows, or ought to know, would cause alarm or distress. It is not an exclusive definition and so other types of conduct can amount to harassment. By a course of conduct, there must be two more or more incidents. It is clear from the cases that, in order to be considered as harassment, the conduct must be of a severe nature. Not every type of irritation or inconvenience can amount to harassment. The conduct has to be sufficiently severe to cross the line and amount to harassment. To a large degree, this will depend on the circumstances of each case. It may be difficult to describe but that hypothetical "reasonable person" in possession of all the facts should be able to recognise it.

Chapter 3

Debt Collectors and Their Lack of Powers

We have probably all seen the letter that comes out from a credit control department, "if the sum is not paid within 7 days, we will pass the account to debt collectors who will call at your door and seize your goods." These types of letters usually go on to describe all the enforcement horrors that will happen if payment is not made. As was mentioned in the previous chapter, the next letter from the debt collection company will threaten all sorts of legal action. These letters tend to give the impression that debt collectors have greater powers in the form of legal action and seizing goods than they actually do. The other misleading aspect of these debt collection letters is that they seem to ignore the fact that, in many of the cases, a court judgment has not been obtained. Without a court judgment, no enforcement will legally follow. Even with a judgment, the creditor will need to apply to court and pay the appropriate court fee to initiate the chosen method of enforcement, such as a warrant of execution, for a county court bailiff, a third party debt order, charging order or whatever type of 'enforcement' is selected. Strictly speaking, a charging order is not a method of enforcement, it secures a debt and you can then pursue an Order for Sale. Much of the language used in these 'Letters before Legal Action' refer to 'Issuing a County Court Judgment'. It is a claim that is issued and if no response is filed at court, or the defence does not succeed at a hearing, then Judgment can be entered.

The term "bailiff" was replaced by the term "enforcement agent" when the provisions in the Tribunal Courts and Enforcement Act 2007 were implemented during April 2014. The main changes introduced by the new provisions include:

1. Bailiffs will be known as Enforcement Agents

2. Enforcement Agents must follow a three stage process:
   i) **Compliance stage** - Upon receipt of an instruction the Enforcement Agent must give the defaulter a minimum of seven clear days notice that he intends to visit their premises to take control of goods.
   ii) **Enforcement stage** - The Enforcement Agent attends apremises to take control of goods and all associated activities prior to the removal of goods for sale.
   iii) **Sale stage** - The Enforcement Agent attends a premises to either remove the goods for the purposes of sale, or commences preparation for sale if the sale is to be held on the premises. This stage concludes when the property is sold or disposed of.

3. Levy, distress and walking possession agreements are replaced by "the process of taking control of goods" and a "controlled goods agreement".
4. There is a time limit of 12 months for taking control of goods but if a payment arrangement is entered into then the 12 month period stops. A full 12 month period re-starts if the payment arrangement defaults.
5. Enforcement Agents may visit premises on any day of the week, including Sundays, but only between the hours of 6am and 9pm. They will not be allowed to enter **homes where only children are present.**
6. Enforcement Agents now have a duty to identify vulnerable persons and refer them to seek advice.
7. Enforcement Agents may take control of 'tools of the trade' with a value in excess of £1,350.00.

8. Enforcement Agents must provide written notice to both the defaulter and any co-owner in respect of any objects over which they have taken control.

9. It will become an offence to interfere with controlled goods or to obstruct an Enforcement Agent in the legal course of their duties.

Enforcement officers do not have the power to force entry to residential premises apart from a few exceptions to recover unpaid fines administered in the Magistrates Courts. These powers do not apply to the collection of unpaid council tax, unpaid parking charges, unpaid congestion charges and unpaid CSA arrears. Her Majesty's Revenue and Customs also have powers that enable them to force entry to premises. An enforcement officer can use reasonable force to enter residential premises if they have gained peaceful entry to the premises on a previous occasion and took control of goods and they are returning to remove the items.

If an Enforcement Officer has taken control of goods within residential premises, *after* gaining peaceful entry, then, if you do not pay, they can use reasonable force to gain entry to remove those goods in order to sell them.

Another aspect which the ordinary member of the public will not necessarily realise when being chased by debt collectors is that the threats of taking legal proceedings are sometimes misleading in that the letters seem to imply that the debt collectors will themselves be issuing proceedings or that they have instructed a lawyer to take court action. In light of a few recent scandals involving banks and loan companies sending letters from - what appeared to be - law firms, when those law firms did not exist, emphasizes the important point that litigation is a "reserved activity" which means that it can only be carried out by those authorised to do so. Section 12 of the Legal Services Act 2007 defines what is meant by a "reserved activity":

12. Meaning of "reserved legal activity" and "legal activity"
(1) In this Act "reserved legal activity" means-

(a) the exercise of a right of audience;
(b) the conduct of litigation;
(c} reserved instrument activities;
(d) probate activities;
(e) notarial activities;
(f) the administration of oaths

Section 12 then goes on to define, for the purposes of the Act, a legal activity as either a reserved legal activity or as the provision of legal advice, assistance or representation in connection with the application of the law or with any form of resolution of legal disputes. Legal activity does not include acting as a mediator or arbitrator. Only an authorised person or an exempt person can carry out a reserved legal activity. It is otherwise a crime to carry out a reserved activity, though it is a defence that the person "did not know, and could not reasonably have been expected to know" that they were committing an offence. It is also an offence to pretend to be authorised. An offender can be sentenced on summary conviction to up to six months imprisonment and a fine of up to £5,000. If convicted on indictment in the Crown Court, an offender can be sentenced to up to two years imprisonment and an unlimited fine. An unauthorised person who purports to exercise a right of audience also commits a contempt of court for which he can be punished.

Authorised persons are either:

- Persons authorised in respect of a given legal activity by a relevant approved regulator; or
- Licensed bodies authorised in respect of those activities.

The term "Lawyer" in England & Wales refers to legally qualified persons that include barristers, solicitors, chartered legal executives and licensed conveyance professionals who are authorised persons to carry out reserved activities.

43

Before the coming into force of the Legal Services Act 2007, lawyers in England and Wales could only practice as:

- Solicitors, as sole traders or in partnerships with other solicitors;
- Barristers, as sole traders; or
- Employees providing legal services to their employer.

The Legal Services Act allows alternative business structures (ABSs) with non-lawyers in professional, management or ownership roles. This is the so-called "Tesco Law" which effectively means that a big company may decide to own a stake in a legal practice. The Act creates a system whereby approved regulators can authorise licensed bodies to offer reserved legal services.

Debt collectors are not authorized to carry out litigation which, as explained above, is a "reserved activity". So the debt collection company will have to instruct a person who has the right to conduct litigation. What undoubtedly happens is that debt collection companies prepare court papers for clients but get the client to sign the Statement of Truth[10]. On the claim form the debt collection company will probably put their address. Sometimes, the Debt Collection Company will sign the Claim Form as "litigation friend". They are wrong on both counts. Schedule 2 of the Legal Services Act 2007 defines what the "conduct of litigation" means:

4. Conduct of litigation
(1) The "conduct of litigation" means:
(a) the issuing of proceedings before any court in England and Wales,
(b) the commencement, prosecution and defence of such proceedings, and
(c) the performance of any ancillary functions in relation to such proceedings (such as entering appearances to actions).

---

[10] The statement of truth is a declaration that the contents of the court form are true.

(2) But the "conduct of litigation" does not include any activity within paragraphs (a) to (c) of sub-paragraph (1), in relation to any particular court or in relation to any particular proceedings, if immediately before the appointed day no restriction was placed on the persons entitled to carry on that activity.

Undoubtedly, the debt collection company will charge its client for the service it is providing and, therefore, it is fair to say that they are performing "ancillary" functions. The dictionary definition of "ancillary" includes "subsidiary" and "assisting". A lawyer who prepares a court document for the client will usually get the client to sign the statement of truth and to say that because the debt collector's client signs the statement of truth they are not litigating is wrong or laying a smoke screen as to what is really going on. It is no doubt the case that some debt collection companies effectively engage in litigation and this is probably a result of their client being unwilling to conduct the court action themselves or pay the costs of solicitors to do it on their behalf.

There have, recently, been examples of where organisations have been sending out letters that appear to come from an independent firm of lawyers but the law firm does not actually exist; in fact, the letter has merely been sent by another department within the same organisation. The Solicitors Regulation Authority is considering issuing guidance for in-house solicitors to make it clear that they cannot use a forms of words that gives the impression they are an independent law firm and not employed solicitors.

In many situations, where a debt is below the small claims limit of £10,000, the types of activity such as litigation - when not authorised to do so - and sending letters that may create the impression of coming from an authorised law firm is, perhaps, understandable as in many cases the debt is not disputed and the debtor is simply not paying what he acknowledges is due. However, this type of action is unlawful. The problem with non-lawyers engaging in litigation is that it can often lead to cases that are relatively straightforward becoming longer and more involved than is proportionate because non-lawyers misunderstand the key points and so are not able to narrow the issues which would reduce the amount of time spent in court.

SUMMARY

Debt collectors do not have the powers that they would like to portray. Even bailiffs do not have that many powers when it comes to trying to take control of goods, for example they cannot force entry into residential premises. When it comes to taking legal proceedings, references made by debt collection companies to the fact that they are going to issue legal proceedings can be misleading as under the Legal Services Act 2007, only the litigant or an authorised person (a lawyer) can conduct litigation.

Chapter 4

Practical Advice to Deal With Harassment

When being hounded by debt collectors for something which you do not owe or genuinely cannot afford to pay, you might be stressed by the intimidating situation and often people will agree to something which is unwise or impracticable. It is easy to say that you should calmly take advice or say "no" but, difficult though it will be in many situations, it is the first step to take.

Debt collectors will be keen to get you to agree to something as they will see this as an admission and will have an arrangement which they can use to exert pressure. It is to their advantage if they can get you to agree to something because they are stepping over the difficult problem they will have if a debtor calmly and logically states the reasons for disputing a debt. The reality is that the debt collector does not want to deal with, or does not have the capacity to deal with, disputed debts. They want to receive from their clients "clean debts" because the requirements, as expressed by the Regulatory Guidelines, to put a matter on hold whilst a dispute is being investigated, is inconvenient for them. A debt collector might be working on a percentage of any recovered debt and if it is referred back to the client then it might result in the instruction being withdrawn or perhaps the client regarding the DCA as weak or inefficient.

If you dispute a claim for money, it is vital to put in writing the reasons why you dispute it. With modern technology, it is easy to communicate in a variety of written forms, such as old-fashioned hard copy letter, e-mail, fax or even text. As I have indicated earlier, the purpose of this book is not to assist those who know they legitimately owe what is being claimed but to assist in presenting a well set out defence to a claim which you genuinely believe you do not owe. The type of claims that are being pursued in a typical debt collecting merry-go-round situation could be getting close to crossing the line into harassment. From my experience, the ordinary person often responds to it in a manner that does not present their case in the best possible way. They are inclined to get caught up in the emotion of the case and drift into obsessive behaviour which leads to the writing of long and rambling letters that do not make the relevant points. What needs to be remembered is that, if the claim being pursued by the creditor is elevated to court action then what you have written will be part of the documents that will be seen at the court hearing. So, not only it is important to write letters that can be clearly understood, you should also consider the tone of such letters. It is very tempting to be rude and sarcastic in such letters but later on when you are reliant upon these documents, for example, at a small claims hearing, the nature of such letters might be a tad embarrassing.

There is also the tendency for the layperson, when responding to a letter of claim by a creditor or other debt collector, to go rather over the top in referring to various pieces of legislation and regulatory matters they claim are being breached. Most of these letters are probably been cobbled together from the vast array of consumer forums that exist and provide template letters for their members to use in order to fend off the attacks from creditors and debt collectors. The problem that I see in some of these cases is that there is too much focus on using a standard template response; I am sure that many large institutions and debt collectors are aware that these letters are fairly standard. I believe that sometimes such long and rambling responses which seem to quote every piece of law since the Magna Carta create the impression that the person defending the claim is slightly mad! The person is most likely aggrieved but, by displaying seemingly obsessive tendencies, the merits of their case and their strongest arguments become rather obscured. So, in some ways I believe that the debt collectors and creditors are perhaps more likely to persist with their claim if they get the impression that the alleged debtor is presenting a load of rambling nonsense because they may not look closely at the real issues and simply dismiss the respondent as being slightly barmy. Therefore, it is important to carefully consider the contents of any letters that are written and not get carried away with irrelevant issues. There is also a need to keep matters in perspective and not overreact before there is a real situation of harassment. This is in keeping with the earlier comments about what constitutes harassment and that the courts have explained that a course of conduct needs to be severe before it crosses the line and becomes harassment.

It may sound obvious advice but avoid having a detailed discussion with the debt collector as to the reasons why you dispute a debt. Not only are the chances of speaking again with the same individual fairly remote, and thus requiring you to explain the whole thing over again to a different person, but there is the danger of you being misunderstood or they will put pressure on you to agree to something you do not want to consent to or would be well advised not to agree.

As someone who is experienced in the telephone technique of persuading other people to pay a debt, I believe that if I could engage the person in conversation and slowly wind them up then I stood a good chance of extracting payment. The skill of a debt collector is to ease back sufficiently to keep the conversation going long enough until you hear the magic words, "I agree to pay". In some cases, you will recognise that they are not going to make any offers and, at that point, you can step up the rudeness provoking them to hang up. I previously thought that if the conversation ended fairly dramatically, or you included some memorable phrases, then that increased the chances of getting payment. Such a conversation would linger longer in the minds of the debtor and would probably lead to either payment to get me off their back or produce further correspondence which might contain some careless admission in an open letter.

The start of the merry-go-round will often be a standard letter received from the credit control department or their debt collecting company. Assuming that the credit control section sends you the letter demanding payment, it is advisable to take a degree of care to ensure that you respond fully and politely to this initial contact. The importance of so doing becomes apparent later and provides you with the solid foundations for your subsequent actions - if needed. To use a cricketing metaphor, it is probably best not to attack too early in your innings; better to play yourself in and get an understanding of what you are dealing with.

Suppose you are the customer or ex-customer of an electricity supply company. You receive a letter saying that you owe a huge amount on your bill. You know that this has nothing to do with you as the meter number is not the same as the one at your premises plus the fact you have evidence of having paid your bill. However, the credit controllers at the electricity supply company still believe it is due and you receive a letter threatening to disconnect you if you do not settle the account within 7 days. Having studied the letter more closely, you realise that the bill relates to a different property. Your address is 25 Boundary Close, Upton, UP10 3BX but there is a 25 Boundary Road, Clifford Village, Nr Upton, UP10 3RR. The village of Clifford is near Upton and you occasionally get letters that are intended for the other address - especially if they do not include "Clifford Village" in the address.

The temptation here would be to simply dial the call centre, listen to that pleasant holding music and have a good rant at the person you speak to who is probably watching the sun set on the Asian continent; far better to write a simple and straight forward letter explaining the fact that you are not responsible for the bill. It is important to get this letter noticed. An e-mail is a quick and cheap method of communicating but the usual contact e-mail address will probably receive hundreds if not thousands of messages plus all the usual spam advertising. Sending an e-mail is probably only worthwhile if you have somebody's direct e-mail address and that person is at a suitable level of authority. Therefore, in such situations, other written forms of communicating where a human being has to physically pick something up by hand is probably likely to grab the recipient's attention. However, beware of certain fax numbers starting 0871, as these are often received by e-mail. If you cannot find a fax, find the registered office of the company and send by recorded delivery to a director, but take the effort to find the name of a director and address it to him/her personally. So far, this all sounds pretty simple and basic advice. As is always the case in the debt collection merry go round, rarely will a mistake be rectified by the customer writing a polite letter pointing out the error. What will follow, as sure as night follows day, is the eager young "telephone collector" who will give you a call, probably at an inconvenient time, to follow up their standard letter chasing payment of a debt which you do not owe.

Having laid the foundations, by responding to the letter demanding payment, you can now start to have a bit of fun with the "telephone collector". Without sounding too smug, you can briefly say that you explained in your letter of X date that you do not owe £X because why would you pay the bill on someone else's meter? The call centre person in this first conversation will pretend to take careful contemporaneous notes and promise solemnly to look into the matter. It is a reasonable assumption that the telephone collector will do no such thing and is probably surfing the net as they speak to you; in a few days you will receive the start of a barrage of calls demanding payment and having no knowledge or record of the previous conversation in which they supposedly noted the nature of your dispute. This would be a breach of Regulatory Guidelines which is the failure to cease collection activity when a debtor raises a reasonable query or dispute.

It is pretty certain at this point that the utility company will pass your account to a debt collection company and send the usual letter threatening all sorts of gloom if the debt is not paid. I could name the usual suspects but I don't want to engage in naming and shaming, as I feel that it is not professional and I wonder whether some would actually feel any shame. This flood of activity is the green light for you to raise your game and to start to play a few attacking shots.

At this point, where you have started to receive a flood of communication after raising a genuine dispute, the appropriate action to take is to send a letter to both the debt collection company and the utility company along the following lines:

> *Dear Sirs*
> **RE: Alleged debt of £_____**
> **Your reference _____**
>
> *I write concerning the frequent contact I have been receiving in respect of the above amount which I do not owe.*
>
> *You claim that this is the amount due in respect of gas supplied with a meter number _____. The reason I dispute this debt is that this meter is not at my property (25 Boundary Close, Upton, UP10 3BX) and I have receipts for the gas I have paid for. Your bills are addressed to "25 Boundary Road, Clifford Village, Nr Upton, UP10 3RR". This is an entirely different property two miles away. Also, the meter and account numbers are different. I have pointed this out to you by recorded delivery letter dated the xx/xx/xx for which you signed for and so you definitely received it. I also told your credit control section on the telephone on the xx/xx/xx this information and they said they would look into the matter. By continuing collection activity before responding to the dispute is a breach of the FCA guidelines. Since then, I have received several telephone calls from you and the debt collection company, you have instructed, demanding payment without any acknowledgment or response to my dispute.*
>
> *I have made my position clear in that it is not my debt. You have produced no evidence to the contrary. If I receive any further contact from you I will regard it as harassment and will consider taking the appropriate legal action under the Protection from Harassment Act 1997. I also notice that you hold a consumer credit licence. If I get any further*

correspondence from you then I will also contact the Financial Conduct Authority (FCA) and ask them to investigate and consider imposing sanctions.

If you believe that I owe the money claimed, then you should issue a claim to in the county court and let a judge decide if the money is due instead of bombarding me with demands for payment.

Yours faithfully,
Fred Smith

In a large number of cases the above letter will provide a sufficient fright that they will stop contacting you. With a bit of luck, you would have brought the merry-go-round to a complete halt or at least made its activities so intermittent that you are no longer concerned by it.

However, there will still be times when such action does not stop the merry-go-round and you will continue to receive letters and telephone calls simply demanding payment with no attempt to answer the legitimate dispute. Chasing a gas bill for a meter which is not yours is certainly a valid dispute. So what do you do to get some acknowledgment from the gas company? Experience suggests that you search for the name of the chief executive or at least find a contact number/address for the top person's office. This may eventually provoke a response. If you chose to take this course of action, enclose a copy of your first letter as the chances are the gas company will have lost the letter or pretend they never received it. It is also important to attempt to get a response because, in the event that you have to take court action to stop the harassment, you can show the court that you tried everything to avoid wasting the court's time. The letter to the chief executive might read something along the following lines:

Dear Sir/Madam,

RE: Disputed Bill
Your reference: _____

I refer to my letter dated _____ , a copy of which is enclosed for ease of reference. I have not received a reply and I am still receiving several telephone calls each week and letters from 2 debt collecting companies.

I am becoming increasingly alarmed by the incessant activity from debt collectors for something which was acknowledged, during a telephone conversation with your meter department on _____, is not my responsibility.

I am particularly alarmed to have received a Notice of your intention to seek a Warrant to disconnect my supply, to be heard at Newton Magistrates Court on xx/xx/xx. I am not able to attend this hearing, as I am working; I do not see why I should be inconvenienced and take time off work to highlight your company's incompetence.

Please confirm within 7 days that this application for a Warrant will be withdrawn and all activities concerning bills that do not relate to me will cease.

Yours faithfully
Fred Smith

This letter to the chief executive's office does finally provoke a response and they confirm that the Warrant application will be withdrawn. Without being too cynical, I would say that, sometimes, the responses you get from the chief executive are standard replies and they may not have personally written the reply. However, if you do manage to get the attention of a person in the organisation who has rather more authority than the debt collector who is writing to you or making telephone calls, there is a better prospect of getting the actions against you stopped.

However, a few weeks pass and the debt collection merry-go-round resumes. Telephone calls are received every day and letters chasing this so called debt arrive from not two but three different debt collection companies. What do you do now? At this point there would appear to be a variety of options:

1. Contact the appropriate Ombudsman
2. Contact the newspapers
3. Apply to a court for an injunction

Ombudsmen investigate and resolve complaints about public and private organisations. The majority of recognised ombudsman schemes are set up by statute; others are voluntary - non-statutory - schemes set up due to the initiative of the service providers concerned. Services provided by insurance companies, banks and building societies are all covered by the Financial Ombudsman Service ("FOS"). As many debt collecting merry-go-round scenarios involve banks and financial institutions, it seems appropriate to consider the work of the FOS. The FOS website [11] outlines what it can do for the consumer:-

"Financial Services Ombudsman

The ombudsman has official powers to settle financial complaints you can't sort out yourself.

We look at the facts, ask questions, and decide what's fair in each individual case. If we uphold your complaint, we can order the business you've complained about to put things right.

---

[11] www.financial-ombudsman.org.uk

The Financial Ombudsman Service is completely independent - and our complaints service is free for consumers.

We can look at complaints about most financial matters including:

* *banking*
* *insurance*
* *mortgages*
* *pensions*
* *savings and investments*
* *credit cards and store cards*
* *loans and credit*
* *hire purchase and pawn broking*
* *money transfer*
* *financial advice*
* *stocks, shares, unit trusts and bonds.*

If you're not sure if we can help with your particular problem - just contact us and ask. Call us on 0300 123 9 123.

We aim to settle complaints as fairly and as quickly as we can. There are always two sides to any complaint, so we'll look carefully at both sides of the story and weigh up all the facts.

If we decide the business you are complaining about has treated you fairly, we will tell you why.

If we decide the business has acted wrongly and you've lost out as a result, we can order the business to put things right for you. Generally, the aim is to put you in the position you'd be in if things hadn't gone wrong.

This can include telling the business to compensate you for losses of up to £100,000. But most complaints involve much smaller amounts than this."

If the consumer accepts the decision of the FOS then it becomes binding on the business and the consumer. If the consumer does not accept the decision then the consumer is able to take their complaint to court.

Using an Ombudsman scheme may be an appropriate way of resolving a dispute but I do come across situations where, despite the decision being accepted by the parties involved, the business continues to pursue the customer as though nothing has happened. A particular example of this was where a customer was being chased for a gas bill they disputed and so referred the matter to the Energy Ombudsman. After an investigation a finding was made in favour of the consumer. However, a few weeks later, the energy company returned to the debt collection merry-go-round and the customer was faced with telephone calls and letters chasing a debt which it had been decided and accepted was not due.

Despite such cases of organisations ignoring the decisions of Ombudsman it is still an avenue worth considering especially in a climate of there we hear news stories of a particular Regulator imposing fines for unacceptable behaviour.

Approaching the newspapers can be an effective method of bringing a halt to the debt collection merry-go-round. Many national papers have a regular column which investigates consumer injustices. In order to avoid further embarrassment, when they receive contact from the journalist the company will often resolve the complaint and offer more compensation than the paltry amount that was originally on the table. With newspapers being prepared to publish articles highlighting the absurdity of such cases, there may be a tendency for some consumers to think that the publicity is a substitute for a lack of substance to the complaint. By this I mean that some people are tempted to use the press to take advantage of media hype and thus disguise the fact that the merits of their case are weak. Of course, to a certain extent, you cannot guard against the bad side of human nature but using the press could work against the person with a stronger case because sometimes a newspaper article misquotes you or puts an unfavourable slant on your case; there is always this danger, when giving your story to a newspaper, unless you have strict control over the contents. However, the newspaper may not publish the article if it cannot put its own slant on the story; that is the freedom of the press in a democratic society.

The last resort to end the debt collection merry-go-round is to take court action in order to obtain an injunction and claim damages for the harassment. As will be discussed later, the level of damages will not be a pot of gold unless the course of conduct is intensive and continues over a prolonged period of time.

The example of Fred Smith trying to get the gas company to realise that the debt was not his responsibility is one type of case that features a lot in the debt collecting merry-go-round. Another common situation is where debt collectors will simply not accept that a person does not have the means to pay the debt or to pay at the rate the creditor wants. It is good advice in this situation to attend your local Citizens Advice Bureau, or contact a body recognised by the creditor (such as Step Change) and complete a comprehensive income and expenditure sheet; an example of one is shown below. This will calculate your disposable income. It would also be prudent to support the financial statement with bank statements, wage slips and, if you are in receipt of any state benefits, the most recent letter showing your entitlement.

See overleaf for the sample financial statement for Fiona Jones.

FINANCIAL STATEMENT OF:	DATE:
Fiona Jones	01-January-2011

Number in Household:	1	Child's age/s:	
This is:			

INCOME		PRIORITY CREDITORS		
Wages/Salary	1000.00	Carried Forward		940.00
Benefits			ARREARS	PAYMENT
Pensions		Rent/Mortgage arrears	400.00	20.00
Other Income		Parish Rates	800.00	25.00
TOTAL INCOME	1000.00	Gas		
		Electricity		
EXPENDITURE		Water	250.00	10.00
Rent/Mortgage	450.00	Other Utilities - Telephone		
Parish Rates	50.00	Other Secured Loans		
Service Charges		Court Fines		
Water Charges	35.00	Wage Arrest		
House Contents Insurance		Maintenance\Child Support		
Life Insurance		TOTAL	1450.00	995.00
Gas	35.00			
Electricity	25.00	INCOME	£1,000.00	
Coal		EXPENDITURE	£995.00	
Oil		Available for		
Telephone		other CREDITORS	£5.00	
Mobile telephone	20.00			
TV Licence	15.00			
HP/Conditional Sale		CREDITOR	BALANCE	OFFER
Housekeeping	120.00	Big UK Bank	2000.00	5
Clothing/footwear	20.00			
Childcare				
Pet food/Vet				
School meals/expenses				
TV/Video				
Health costs				
Car costs - petrol	100.00			
Car costs - insurance	20.00			
Car costs - parking	30.00			
Subscriptions and outings				
Bus Fares				
Haircuts				
Miscellaneous	20.00			
TOTAL	940.00	TOTAL	2000.00	5

I/We confirm that this is a true reflection on my/our financial situation   Signed

ADDITIONAL COMMENTS:

The financial statement of Fiona Jones shows that she has a monthly disposable income of £5. She is 22, works 35 hours per week and is paid not much more than the national minimum wage in respect of her hourly rate. She is being chased by Big UK Bank for a £2,000 personal loan. She sends the following letter to the recovery department at Big UK Bank:

Dear Sirs,

My Loan Account Number: 22872291/2010
Amount Outstanding: £2,000

I write regarding my outstanding loan account.

I have been to Citizen's Advice Bureau and completed a comprehensive financial statement. Enclosed with this financial statement are documents in support of my position including 3 months wage slips and bank statements to show my income, as well as documents showing my expenditure, including my tenancy agreement and other copy bills. I do not own any property and have no savings.

My present financial position is that I have disposable income of only £5 per month and I put forward this offer to pay the outstanding loan with Big UK Bank. I realise that this is a small sum per month but this is all that I can afford at present. I would suggest that the level of repayment is reviewed in 6 months time when hopefully my financial situation will have improved.

I look forward to your response
Yours faithfully

The response Fiona receives is quite surprising, but experience shows that this does happen:

Dear Madam,

Re: Your Loan Account
Reference: 22872291/2010

We refer to your letter of xx/xx/xx along with enclosures.

We note that you do not have funds at the moment to pay this loan but unless we receive an acceptable offer collection activity will continue........

Following this letter, Fiona receives 6 calls per day on her mobile telephone, a letter each week from the collections department, as well as letters from Collections R-Us Ltd and Ace Collectors Ltd. You may think that Fiona should simply turn off her mobile telephone. However, she has a an elderly mother and she could receive a call at any time to say she is not well, but in any case, why should she have to turn off her phone? Big UK Bank has options if they do not accept this offer. They could issue legal action, obtain a judgment and let a court decide the rate of payment. As this is a consumer debt and Fiona has produced a detailed financial statement, it is very unlikely that a district judge would order a higher rate of payment. If the bank believes that Fiona is not revealing her true financial position it could obtain judgment and then request an order to attend court for questioning or employ an enquiry agent to look into her finances. Alternatively, it could issue a bankruptcy petition but this would be costly and, as they are an unsecured creditor, it would be unlikely to yield any return for the bank as she has no assets.

On her visit to the CAB, Fiona Jones would have received advice about her possible entitlement to benefits such as working tax credits. The website www.turn2us.org.uk contains a useful calculator to assess your entitlement to benefits. Also, faced with debt, Fiona should receive advice as to whether it would be worth considering bankruptcy or some other form of debt relief such as a debt relief order (DRO) or an individual voluntary arrangement

61

(IVA). In particular circumstances, it might be appropriate for the individual to pursue one of these options but it is not the intention of this book to give advice as whether or not to go bankrupt or seek one of the alternatives such as a DRO or IVA. The advice would certainly make clear the consequences of bankruptcy or the alternatives and for this reason Fiona Jones decides not to follow one of these options. Although Fiona is not earning much as present, she has qualifications and is expecting to obtain a better job in the next few years and does not want her credit rating blighted by personal insolvency.

If Big UK Bank, at this point, does not take court action but, instead, continues its collection activities in the form of constant phone calls and letters, it would clearly be harassment and a breach of section 40 of the Administration of Justice Act 1970, because the only purpose of such continued contact would be to coerce her into paying more than she can afford. As a last resort, Fiona could consider taking legal action to seek an injunction and damages for harassment. Before commencing court action it would be advisable to write one final letter to Big UK Bank along the lines set out below in order to protect her position on costs should the case proceed to a trial. As has been mentioned, the courts expect parties to consider ADR. An unreasonable refusal not to consider alternative methods of settling may mean the court could reflect this when it comes to making a costs order. In reality, what this could mean is that the winner of the case may not get all of their costs as the court may consider the litigation was unnecessary.

Dear Sir/Madam,

RE: _____

I am disappointed that you have not responded positively to my letter of xx/xx/xx. I have made an offer which is all that I can presently afford. You have stated in your letter that you acknowledge I do not have the funds but will continue collection activity until I make an acceptable offer. This to me sounded like you intended to harass and coerce me into paying more than I can afford. In fact, that is what has happened in that I have received at least 6 calls per day and several letters per week from not only your collections department but from 2 debt collection companies.

I am finding that this constant communication from you and your agents is making me increasingly anxious. I would ideally turn my phone off to avoid these calls but I need to be contactable because I have an elderly mother but in any case, why should have I have to turn it off?

If you do not believe that my offer of repayment is reasonable, then you have the option to take legal action and let a court decide whether the offer is reasonable. If you continue with the course of conduct (which any reasonable person would regard as harassment) then I will start court proceedings and seek an injunction as well as claim damages. I would obviously wish to avoid court action and suggest that a senior manager from your organisation arranges to meet me to discuss the matter. If you are not prepared to discuss this and you continue to harass me, then I will take court action.

Yours sincerely

Fiona Jones

Fiona does not get a response to this letter but instead she continues to receive calls demanding that she pays more that she has offered. In this situation it would be appropriate to consider taking court action.

We have seen in the earlier case study where a utility company fails to understand that the person they are chasing is not responsible for the debt and when the debt collector is asked for documentation to support the fact that they claim the money is

63

due; nothing is forthcoming except repeated demands for payment. If they refuse to provide the information and do take steps to issue court action then there are various provisions which you can use in order to suspend the action until the creditor provides the information. It is often the debts which have been sold which are the ones where the debt collectors are not able to provide the answers or all of the relevant documents because, sometimes, the sale of the debt took place a long time ago and many of the documents may no longer exist or are difficult to locate. Chapter 1 mentioned the case of Mr Evans and OK Energy. In that situation, the issue was that Mr Evans was asking on what basis OK Energy were permitted to charge what in effect is a cancellation fee or a higher rate when giving notice to move to another supplier. The issue here is whether or not such a term was incorporated into the contract, i.e. forms part of the contract. If OK Energy issues proceedings and the Particulars of Claim do not contain any more information on this point, Mr Evans should follow certain procedural avenues to get OK Energy to detail their claim. Supposing the Particulars of Claim is as follows:

"The Claim is for the price of electricity charged between xx/xx/xx and a charge for the termination of the contract. The Claimant claims the sum of £11,000 plus interest pursuant to section 69 of the County Courts Act 1984."

Mr Evans disputes the claim. He first files an acknowledgement of service, within 14 days of service of the claim form, stating his intention to defend. This means that he will have 28 days from the date of service within which to file his full defence. He should ask the Claimant to consider granting extra time in which to prepare his defence and a request for further information. If OK Energy refuses to grant extra time, and it is expected that a reasonable period should be granted, Mr Evans would need to make an application to the court. The application should request an extension of time and an Order that the Defendant answer what is called a Part 18 request. It is called this because CPR Part 18 governs this area. A

Part 18 request can only be made in a case that is not in the small claims track as CPR Part 18 does not apply to small claims. A claim will normally be in the small claims track if the claim for money does not exceed £10,000. Where CPR Part 18 is applicable, it states:

Obtaining further information
18.1
(1) The court may at any time order a party to –
(a) clarify any matter which is in dispute in the proceedings; or
(b) give additional information in relation to any such matter,whether or not the matter is contained or referred to in a statement of case.
(2) Paragraph (1) is subject to any rule of law to the contrary.
(3) Where the court makes an order under paragraph (1), the party against whom it is made must –
(a) file his response; and
(b) serve it on the other parties,
within the time specified by the court.
(Part 22 requires a response to be verified by a statement of truth)
(Part 53 (defamation) restricts requirements for providing further information about sources of information in defamation claims)

Restriction on the use of further information
18.2
The court may direct that information provided by a party to another party (whether given voluntarily or following an order made under rule 18.1) must not be used for any purpose except for that of the proceedings in which it is given.

In this case, the request for further information might be as follows:

Question 1:

Is the Claimant relying upon written terms and conditions and conditions?

Answer:

Question 2:

If the Claimant is relying on written terms and conditions, please state the wording of the term that the Claimant alleges permits it to charge a cancellation fee. If the Claimant is relying on an oral term, please provide details of the words spoken to the Defendant.

Answer:

Question 3:

Please detail when and how the terms were brought to the attention of the Defendant.

Answer:

The Response to the Part 18 request must contain a Statement of Truth. It will form part of the Statements of Case, or "pleadings" as they were known.

Small claims where CPR Part 18 does not apply

Cases that are in the small claims track follow a modified court procedure where certain parts of the court rules do not apply; part 18 of the CPR is one such rule that does not apply to the small claims track. Even though in small claims Part 18 does not apply, there is every benefit in putting questions to the creditor if the particulars of claim are especially brief and further information is required.

Debts that have been purchased

The opening chapter highlighted the fact that debt sale is a big contributor to the debt collecting merry-go-round. This can often lead to debt purchasers chasing debts that are often quite old and the fact that the seller of the debt will usually not be too concerned about providing information once the debt has been sold makes the collection of the debt increasingly difficult. This should be borne in mind by the person being chased by the new owner of the debt. Some of the debts are often so old that they may have passed the limitation period. The limitation periods are governed by the Limitation Act 1980. The limitation period for the recovery of a debt is 6 years. Deciding if a debt is outside the limitation period often arises where a debtor has made part payments and there has been a long gap since the last payment. Under section 29 of the Limitation Act 1980, acknowledging a debt or making part payment has the effect of renewing the limitation period from the date of acknowledgment or payment. So, for example, if a debt became due in April 2003, and a part payment is made in April 2007, then instead of the limitation period expiring in April 2009, the limitation will be renewed on the making of the payment in 2007 and the limitation period will expire in May 2013. Under section 30, any acknowledgment must be in writing signed by the person liable or by that person's agent. However, part payment of rent or interest due at any time does not extend the time for claiming the balance.

It is likely that debt purchase companies will be pursuing debts that are fairly old and quite close to the expiration of the limitation period. Sometimes the debt will be statute barred (beyond the expiration of the limitation period) but the debt purchaser will not have accurate information as to what has been paid. In this situation, it is reasonable to require the debt purchaser to produce proof that the debt is still within the limitation period. Remember, the burden of proof falls upon the Claimant - in a civil action - to demonstrate, on the balance of probability, that the debt is due.

Debt purchase companies will write to the debtor announcing that their debt has been an assigned to them, i.e. the debt has been sold to them by the original creditor. It is significant to know whether there was a "legal" assignment or an "equitable" assignment. Under the Law of Property Act 1925, the requirements of a legal assignment are as follows:

- Only the benefit can be assigned
- The assignment must be absolute (transferred unconditionally).
- The rights must be ascertainable (must not relate to only part of the debt)
- The assignment must be in writing and signed by the assignor (the creditor selling the debt)
- Notice must be received by the other party for the assignment to take effect.

If it does not meet the requirements of a legal assignment then it may take effect as an equitable assignment. The key difference between a legal and equitable assignment is that an assignee (the person to whom the debt has been assigned) cannot bring an action on their own but must join in the assignor (the person who assigned the debt) into any court proceedings. This could be important because if the assignment is equitable and court proceedings are required, it is unlikely that the company which assigned the debt would want to be involved in such proceedings.

Where 6 years have elapsed since the date of a judgment, permission is required to enforce it by way of execution (either by writ in the high court or a warrant in the county court). The application to the court will ask the court to exercise its discretion. Whilst exercise of its discretion is directed at doing justice between the parties in all the circumstances of the case, the court will only extend the six-year period where it is demonstrably just to do so. The burden of proof is on the judgment creditor to show that it is just. It should be made clear that this permission is only required where the judgment creditor is seeking to enforce the Judgment after 6 years by way of a writ or warrant of execution, i.e. through a bailiff. This requirement does not apply to other forms of enforcement, i.e. third party debt orders, charging orders or attachment of earnings orders.

There have been attempts to extend the principle to require permission to be obtained with all types of enforcement after 6 years have elapsed since the date of Judgment. When the court considers making an interim third party debt order or interim charging order final, the debtor can, at that stage, make representations as to the fact that there has been considerable delay in taking steps to enforce the Judgment. However, Mr Justice Tomlinson made clear in **Westacre Investments Inc v The State-owned Company Yugoimport [2008],**

> *"In my judgment in the absence of some compelling evidence of prejudice to the judgment debtor accruing from the delay in enforcement, the court would regard the grant of garnishee relief as virtually axiomatic."*

What he meant was that even if an analogy were to be drawn between the specific rules applicable to the issue of a warrant of execution and other forms of enforcement, there would have to be some very significant evidence of delay that has seriously prejudiced the debtor. So, a delay of a few months past the point of 6 years from the date of Judgment is unlikely to be sufficient; it would need to be a case of the creditor making no enforcement attempts whatsoever long after the 6 year period.

SUMMARY

There are a number of things which you can do when faced with a pressing a creditor to slow the pace of the merry-go-round. The steps you ought to take will depend on whether or you admit the debt is due. If the debt is due, then the best course of action is to honestly set your financial position and to make a reasonable proposal to pay in the circumstances. If you owe the money, don't simply bury your head in the sand because with that attitude your whole body will soon slip beneath the dunes and climbing out of the situation becomes more arduous. If there is a genuine dispute then set out clearly in writing the reasons for disputing the debt, including information and documents to support your refusal to pay. If you receive relevant follow up questions in reply to your detailed denial of the debt, then answer those. But if the unwarranted behaviour emerges by way of endless calls and letters simply demanding payment, then that is the signal to say "enough is enough".

Chapter 5

Taking Legal Action to Stop Harassment

This chapter gives guidance on how to take legal action against a debt collector engaging in harassment or other unfair practices. Legal action should be regarded as the last resort. In the previous chapter, we considered practical advice on how to correspond and hopefully avoid arriving at the point at which the only option to stop the intrusion is to take court action. Legal action should not be considered an easy option; proper attention should be given to the merits of the case and the costs involved in bringing the action and the potential award relating to the other side's legal fees if you do not succeed. This book cannot be expected to give a comprehensive answer in respect of every type of case and so you should seek professional legal advice before starting. Admittedly, you might well be unable to afford to pay for such advice but there are a number of law firms that provide legal clinics. When considering the merits of your case it is important to be realistic. It is easy to get swept up in what becomes a crusade to slay the "nasty dragon" that is the big organisation, but remember a court will look at the evidence to decide cases; you will not simply win on sympathy alone. So a claim against a bank, utility company or whomever should not be regarded as an opportunity to have a pop at a sector of society that is not currently very high up in the popularity table.

The following case study of Chris Jones v Big Bank UK Ltd will be used to illustrate how to take appropriate court action.

Mr Chris Jones is a Quantity Surveyor by profession. He borrowed £12,000 from the Big UK Bank Plc. He is never behind with repayments until he loses his job due to redundancy. At this point, there is £8,000 remaining on the loan. Mr Jones finds it hard to maintain the loan repayments. He receives a call from the recovery department of Big UK Bank. Mr Jones writes to Big Bank and provides details of his financial circumstances. He provides a full income & expenditure statement with the assistance of the Citizens Advice Bureau. He then receives a very inadequate response. The bank states that "...although I am aware you have no funds available, I am unable to withhold any action on your account for 6 months." There is further correspondence and Mr Jones is told that calls will continue until an acceptable repayment plan is agreed.

Following this letter, Mr Jones receives numerous calls and texts each day, on some days up to 12 calls. This goes on for a period of 3 months. He notes down the telephones calls and texts which he received in that 3 month period. There may be more but these are the ones he has recorded. The number of calls has been very considerable and on some days he has received a total of 5 calls. The number of calls appears to increase after Mr Jones makes contact and explains that he only has a very small amount of disposable income as he is on Job Seekers Allowance.

Before commencing legal proceedings, you would be expected to send an appropriate letter of claim. The court rules have various pre-action protocols and although there is no specific protocol for this type of claim, the court rules contain a general protocol where no particular one applies. In short, the letter of claim should contain the following:

2. Claimant's letter before claim[12]

2.1
The claimant's letter should give concise details about the matter. This should enable the defendant to understand

---

[12] This an extract from the Pre-action Protocols for cases where no specific protocol applies

and investigate the issues without needing to request further information. The letter should include –
(1) the claimant's full name and address;
(2) the basis on which the claim is made (i.e. why the claimant says the defendant is liable);
(3) a clear summary of the facts on which the claim is based;
(4) what the claimant wants from the defendant;
(5) if financial loss is claimed, an explanation of how the amount has been calculated; and
(6) details of any funding arrangement (within the meaning of rule 43.2(1)(k) of the CPR) that has been entered into by the claimant.

2.2
The letter should also –
(1) list the essential documents on which the claimant intends to rely;
(2) set out the form of ADR (if any) that the claimant considers the most suitable and invite the defendant to agree to this;
(3) state the date by which the claimant considers it reasonable for a full response to be provided by the defendant; and
(4) identify and ask for copies of any relevant documents not in the claimant's possession and which the claimant wishes to see.

2.3
Unless the defendant is known to be legally represented the letter should –
(1) refer the defendant to this Practice Direction and in particular draw attention to paragraph 4 concerning the court's powers to impose sanctions for failure to comply with the Practice Direction; and

(2) inform the defendant that ignoring the letter before claim may lead to the claimant starting proceedings and may increase the defendant's liability for costs.

If you are a layperson and are undertaking legal action on your own behalf, the court would not be too critical if you did not follow the protocol exactly to the letter but they would at least expect you to send a letter before commencing court action which sets out the nature of your claim and giving them a reasonable opportunity to respond. An example of an appropriate letter of claim in the case of Jones and the Big UK Bank is set out below:

Dear Sirs,

FORMAL LETTER OF CLAIM

This is a formal letter of claim for damages and/ or an injunction against your organisation in respect of harassment I have experienced. Please pass this letter to your legal department. I enclose copies of recent correspondence as well as a sheet detailing the number and dates of calls and texts I have received.

Background:

In summary, I wrote to Big Bank on xx/xx/xx following a call on xx/xx/x, setting out my financial circumstances. I provided a full income & expenditure statement with the assistance of the Citizens Advice Bureau. I received a very inadequate response dated xx/xx/xxxx. I then wrote a further detailed letter, of xx/xx/xxxx, within which I make it clear that you have not provided a reasonable response and that the constant telephone calls were causing me distress. In your more detailed response of xx/xx/xxxx, it is stated "..although I am aware you have no funds available to offer, I am unable to withhold any action on your account for 6 months." I received further correspondence and calls and they stated that, until an acceptable repayment plan is agreed, collection activity would continue.

I enclose a sheet detailing the list of telephones calls and texts, which I have received for the three-month period from xx/xx/xxxx until yy/yy/yyyy. The number of calls has been very considerable and on some days I received a total of 5 calls. The number of calls I received seemed to increase after I detailed my financial situation.

The Nature and basis of the claim

I claim that your activities set out above amount to harassment under section 1 of the Protection from Harassment Act 1997 which states that:

"A person must not pursue a course of conduct which amounts to harassment of another, and which he knows or ought to know amounts to harassment of the other".
For the purposes of this section, the person whose course of conduct is in question ought to know that it amounts to harassment of another if a reasonable person in possession of the same information would think the course of conduct amounted to harassment of the other."

Under section 3 of the Act I am entitled to claim damages.

I also submit that you are in breach of section 40 of the Administration of Justice Act 1970 which states that "A person commits an offence if, with the object of coercing another person to pay money claimed from the other as a debt due under a contract, he:

(a) harasses the other with demands for payment which, in respect of their frequency or the manner or occasion of *making any such demand, or of any threat or publicity by which any demand is accompanied, are calculated to subject him or members of his family or household to alarm, distress or humiliation;"*

Further, I believe you are in breach of the Regulatory Guidelines on Debt Collection.

I am seeking

1. An injunction to prevent further debt collection activity.
2. Damages in compensation for the harassment I have suffered.

You should be aware that the courts expect the parties to a dispute to attempt other methods of resolving a dispute. I am happy to enter into mediation/negotiations.

If we are not able to resolve this matter then I will unfortunately have to issue court proceedings and will seek an injunction and damages. I would also draw your attention to the Protocol on Pre-Action Conduct which states that I should receive a full reply within a reasonable period of time which I suggest in this case is 21 days from the date of this letter.

Yours faithfully

Chris Jones

Alternative dispute resolution

When faced with harassment from large organisations in the way Chris Jones has, it will be understandable for you not to even consider any alternative methods of dispute resolution. However, not only is it a possible way of quickly getting an acceptable resolution but if it does progress to legal action then the claimant will receive credit when and if the issue of costs comes to be decided. ADR such as mediation is not a magic wand but in the right circumstances it can be a useful tool. In such a process, the Claimant would be able to express to the other party via the mediator their grievances and such discussions are without prejudice, which means that the contents cannot be relied on later if the court action continues. If a party feels reluctant to meet the other side face-to-face, then having a mediator move backwards and forwards between the parties is good way of making progress towards an agreement without the process degenerating into a slanging match.

The mediator does not make a decision on the merits of the case but tries to bring the parties together to reach a settlement. The skill and purpose of a mediator is to make the parties see their weaknesses which may encourage them to accept a compromise. A mediation may succeed in certain situations, such as where there are particular risks in going to court; this may be where the case is very dependent on oral evidence and the events are some time ago with the recollection of witnesses having faded.

An argument put forward for mediation is that some say it is cheaper. In some cases, this is undoubtedly true but a day of mediation between one individual and a large organisation does front load a fair amount of cost disproportionately on the individual. It may well be that instead of paying a mediator to run back and forth between the parties, it might be better for the parties to simply have a "round table" meeting. If it is made clear that the meeting is "without prejudice", then it is possible to have a full and frank discussion and this may lead to a creative solution being achieved.

Mediation is not the only type of ADR; there is adjudication which might be by an arbitrator, an appointed expert or an Ombudsman. Adjudication has the advantage that a decision on the merits is made. In a case such as Chris Jones, and as it involves a bank, the Financial Ombudsman would be a possible way of resolving the dispute. Whatever method of ADR is considered, the key point that Chris Jones or anyone in this situation should remember is that you should think of the alternatives and not think that court action followed by a trial is inevitable.

In the case of Chris Jones and Big UK Bank, Chris Jones accepts an invitation from the Head of Customer Relations at Big UK Bank, John Doshmore, to a "without prejudice" meeting. The meeting is held at the branch of Big UK Bank that is nearest to Chris Jones.

John Doshmore: Mr Jones, thank you for coming today to discuss your concerns you have with Big UK Bank. Shall we start by you setting out exactly what you are dissatisfied with?

Chris Jones: Well, I would have thought that was pretty clear from my correspondence. I lost my job and fell behind with my loan repayments. I thought I did the correct thing and went to the CAB and sought advice about presenting my financial position to the bank and asking if they would accept a lower repayment until I am back on my feet. However, your bank seems to ignore the fact that I cannot afford to pay anymore at present and instead continue to make constant telephone calls in what can only be described as an attempt to coerce me into paying more. I would say that most reasonable people would view this as harassment.

John Doshmore: Well I am sorry that you feel that you have been harassed by the bank, but obviously we have to try and recover monies which we have loaned.

Chris Jones: Even if those methods are unfair and unlawful?

John Doshmore: Is it unlawful to chase a legitimate debt? You will understand.....

Chris Jones: No, I think you misunderstand. Yes, I accept that I owe the money and have every intention of paying it back but the methods you are using at the moment and the frequency of contact is simply causing me distress at a time I am stressed enough as I do not have a job.

John Doshmore: I note that you have not provided an income and expenditure report through one of our suggested debt adviser organisations....

Chris Jones: What is wrong with the information I provided through the CAB?

John Doshmore: Well, we require you to seek debt management advice from one of the companies on our list because...

Chris Jones: because there is something in it for the bank?!!

John Doshmore: No it's not that, but rather we feel these organisations provide quality advice.

Chris Jones: I think the reputation of the CAB is pretty high and they are independent. Anyway, let me ask you, will the bank stop ringing me 5 times a day and accept that I can only afford £5 per week at the moment as I am on JSA?

John Doshmore: I can't commit to the fact that the bank will not continue to chase for the loan.

Chris Jones: But do you accept that my finances are difficult?

John Doshmore: I understand it is difficult but I cannot say that the collections unit will accept the offer of £5 per week.

Chris Jones: Well, this is what I propose. I will pay £5, per week until I have obtained a job and then will complete a new income and expenditure sheet and increase the payment to reflect the higher disposable income I should have. If you are not prepared to accept this figure of £5 per week then you have the option of taking me to court and getting a court to decide a fair rate of payment. If in the meantime, the bank continues to call me then I will proceed and seek an injunction to stop the constant contact which is really getting me down. To show how much it is getting me down, here is a note from my doctor which shows I consulted him and he said I was suffering from anxiety, made worse by this matter.

John Doshmore: Can I keep this copy of the doctor's note?
Chris Jones: Yes, certainly.
John Doshmore: I will ask the collections team to suspend their activity and I will ask the loans director whether or not they will accept the offer.

The meeting ends with Chris Jones thinking that perhaps a breakthrough had been made and the constant calling will stop. Chris starts and continues to make the payment of £20 per month. In fact, during the next two weeks, he receives no contact from the collections department of Big UK Bank or their debt collection agents. However, it must have been the calm before the storm as during the third week after the meeting with Mr Doshmore, the calls start coming in - thick and fast. He starts receiving calls, not only from Big UK Bank but from 2 debt collection companies "Central Debt Collectors" and "Speedy Collections". In addition to half a dozen telephone calls a day, he receives two letters each week from these companies. Mr Jones has been having several interviews and leaves his phone on as he is anxiously waiting the outcome but all he gets is the aggressive contact from debt collectors. In his mind, enough is enough and he decides to follow through with legal action as he feels he has tried all other avenues.

How to issue a claim under the Protection from Harassment Act 1997

In this situation, Chris Jones would be advised to apply for an interim injunction at the time he issues the claim to try and prevent further contact from the bank until the court decides the issue.

Cases brought under the Protection from Harassment Act 1997 must be commenced in the County Court of the district where the Claimant resides or the High Court. He will need to prepare the following and send it to the Newtown County Court (or the High Court):

- Claim Form N208
- All written evidence in support, including witness statements

If the Claimant signs the statement of truth on the second page of the Claim Form then the contents of the Claim Form may stand as the Claimant's evidence and so you do not necessarily have to file a separate witness statement. In this case, Chris Jones is acting in person and he has signed the Statement of Truth and so the contents of the Claim Form can be used by him as evidence.

- Application for an Interim Injunction in Form N16A and a witness statement in support

Set out below is a completed form N16A by Chris Jones and a sample witness statement in support.

- Draft Order for Interim Injunction

As a layperson, Chris Jones would not be expected to know how to draft the perfect draft order but he has included an outline of the Order he is seeking.

- Court fee or an Application for a Fee Remission

The court fee to issue the claim is £175 and the fee for the interim injunction application is £80, unless Chris Jones qualifies for a fee remission. Chris Jones is on income based job seekers allowance and so he qualifies for a full fee remission.

Completed versions of the forms are shown in Appendix 1. This type of claim and interim application involves points of law and anybody wishing to bring this type of claim is well advised to instruct solicitors or at least seek proper advice before embarking on such action. If you are in the position that Mr Jones is in then you will be concerned about the cost of instructing lawyers.

However, there may well be law firms that would consider taking on this claim on a conditional fee agreement, commonly known as a "no win no fee agreement".

What happens next?

The court will serve the Claim Form and the written evidence of Chris Jones on Big UK Bank Plc. This type of claim proceeds under the rules as set out in Part 8 of the Civil Procedure Rules (CPR). A claim under the Protection from Harassment Act 1997 follows the Part 8 procedure because CPR Part 65.28 states such claims are subject to it. Part 8 applies to certain specified claims and can be used where the claim has no substantial dispute of fact and so to use the normal Part 7 procedure would be unnecessarily cumbersome. CPR Part 7 is the procedure used for most claims and debt actions.

Under the Part 8 procedure, the Defendant has 14 days from the date of service to file the acknowledgement of service in form N210 which is shown at the end of this chapter. The Part 8 procedure does not require the Defendant to file a defence. The acknowledgement of service states whether the defendant contests the claim and if he seeks to rely on witness evidence then this should be filed together with the acknowledgement of service. In practice, 14 days will not be long enough to gather together evidence and so the parties can agree an extension of up to 14 days in which to file written evidence or the defendant can apply to the court for an extension of time in which to file the acknowledgment of service. When filing the acknowledgment of service, the Defendant can object to the use of the Part 8 procedure but must file reasons for opposing the procedure. If the defendant does not file an acknowledgment of service then they will not be able take part in any hearing. However, the claimant cannot request judgment in default if no acknowledgment is filed.

Within 14 days of service of the Defendant's written evidence, the Claimant can file evidence in reply. Part 8 claims are usually allocated to the multi-track and there is no need to complete an allocation questionnaire. The court will then give directions, often listing the claim for a short hearing at which the case management of the claim will be considered. If the defendant has not filed an acknowledgment of service or filed any evidence, then the case might be disposed of at this short hearing. Otherwise, the court will list the claim for a trial and give any other appropriate directions, such as permitting the parties to file any further evidence within 14 days. The other usual directions will be given such as requiring the claimant to prepare a paginated trial bundle 7 days before the trial and the parties to file and serve skeleton arguments 3 days before the hearing.

The likely outcome in Jones v. Big UK Bank Plc

The outcome of a trial is never certain. What has to be remembered is that the trial judge might only read the papers shortly before the trial. Also, the claimant has that one opportunity at the trial to impress the strength of his case upon the Judge. Therefore the result can depend on how well the case comes across on the day.

A client often asks his lawyer for an estimate of their chances of succeeding in percentage terms. This sort of assessment is not easy. Lawyers will most likely be slightly cautious because of the fear of a client being disappointed if the lawyer is too optimistic and possibly being criticised for not advising them correctly. Therefore, lawyers rarely say a case has a better than 70% chance and even a 70% prospect is regarded as high. So lawyers tend to assess prospects as being in the region of 50 to 70%. Of course there will be some cases where lawyers can say that the chances are really good and are greater than 70% but there are not going to be many. A 50% prospect of success may not sound great to a client but when you take account of this cautious approach to assessing prospects of success it puts it in context. However, if you are attempting to obtain legal expenses insurance, the insurance company will usually expect the prospects of success to be at least 60%.

The facts of Chris Jones v Big UK Bank Plc would suggest that he has a very good prospect of proving that the course of conduct by Big UK Bank amounted to harassment. As to the remedy, Chris Jones is likely to be awarded damages but as the case of **Poncelet v NPower**[13] mentions, the calculation of damages is not easy to assess. However, the figure of £5,000 is likely to be a reasonable sum in all of the circumstances. There is also a real prospect that, as the trial approaches, Big UK Bank is likely to attempt to settle this claim out of court to avoid the adverse publicly such a case might create.

If Big UK Bank were to start negotiating a settlement ahead of the trial, Chris Jones would be well advised to conclude an agreement with the signing of a Tomlin Order. A Tomlin Order (named after a case of this name) is a form of consent order whereby the court proceedings are stayed (suspended) on the basis that agreement has been reached and will not be re-started provided the terms of the agreement are carried out. If the terms of agreement are breached, the case is re-instated so that the terms of the agreement can be enforced against the defaulting party.

It should be borne in mind that the bank (or its lawyers) will probably discuss a settlement which they will get Chris to agree and move toward drawing up suitable terms of settlement. It has been known that after the parties have agreed to settle the matter, the bank attempts to slip in strict confidentiality clauses. The desire to have these clauses should be put forward at the time of making the proposal so that if the bank is offering to pay £5,000 to Chris Jones, they should, at the same time, say that this is subject to a confidentiality agreement and state any other conditions of payment including when it will be paid. The reason for flagging this issue is that it is sometimes forgotten that a binding contract is made up of offer and acceptance and so if the bank asks without prejudice whether you will discontinue your claim for £5,000 and you say yes, then strictly speaking it is not then able to say they

---

[13] Full text of the judgment is at Appendix 2

want other terms into an agreement, such as a confidentiality clause. If Chris Jones is asked to agree to a confidentiality clause he would be advised to say that he would consent to clause which says:

"The parties agree to keep the terms of this settlement confidential. For avoidance of doubt, it is not a breach of this agreement to say that this claim is settled."

An appropriate Tomlin Order in this case would read something like the following:

Upon the parties having agreed the terms set out in the schedule below

IT IS ORDERED BY CONSENT:

1. All further proceedings in the claim are stayed except for the purpose of enforcing the terms agreed between the parties
2. The Defendant do pay the costs of the Claimant assessed at £_____within 14 days of the date of this order.
3. Either Party has liberty to apply to enforce the agreed terms.

SCHEDULE

a. The Defendant shall pay the sum of £5,000 (Five Thousand) to the Claimant in settlement of the Claimant's claim against the Defendant. Payment is to be made within 21 days of the date of this agreement.
b. The parties are not to discuss the terms of the settlement with any third party except with their legal advisers and as required to do so by law. For the avoidance of doubt, for a party to mention that the case

85

is settled and no more, is not a breach of this agreement.

c. If the Defendant defaults on its obligations contained within this schedule, the Claimant may request Judgment without further Order.

It is quite likely that Big UK Bank will not want to admit liability for reasons that they do not want the floodgates to open. Therefore, they may want paragraph "a" of the Schedule to be worded differently:

"a. Without admitting liability, the Defendant agrees to pay the sum of £5,000....."

It should not matter because the schedule to a Tomlin Order is not part of the Order. The schedule is an agreement between the parties. Therefore, the Defendant in this situation will often want the schedule to be on a separate sheet attached to the back of the order.

IN THE NEWTOWN COUNTY COURT   **Case No:**

B E T W E E N:

Mr Christopher Jones   **Claimant**

And

Big UK Bank Plc
Defendant

Statement of Christopher Jones

I, CHRISTOPHER JONES, of 10 Canal Road, Newton will say as follows:

1. I make this statement from information within my own knowledge. Where it is not, I state the source of my belief.

2. I am the Claimant in these proceedings. I make this statement in support of my claim for harassment against Big UK Bank PLC and in relation to my application for an interim injunction. I refer to a bundle of documents attached and marked CJ

3. I have one loan outstanding with the Defendant. In total, I owe about £8,000. I am a Quantity Surveyor by profession. I borrowed £12,000 from the Big UK Bank Plc. I was never behind with repayment until I lost my job when the company made me redundant. At this point, there is £8,000 left on the loan. I received a call from the recovery department of Big UK Bank. I wrote to Big Bank and provide details of my financial circumstances.

4. I provided a full income & expenditure statement with the assistance of the Citizens Advice Bureau. I received a very inadequate response. The bank stated that *"...although I am aware you have no funds available to offer, I am unable to withhold any action on your account for 6 months"*. There is further correspondence and I am told that calls will continue until an acceptable repayment plan is agreed. Following this letter, I received numerous calls and texts each day, on some days up to 12 calls. This continued for a period of 3 months. I noted down the telephones calls and texts which I received during that 3

87

month period. The times and dates of the calls are detailed within page ____ of the bundle. There may be more but these are the ones I have recorded. The number of calls has been very considerable and on some days I have received a total of 5 calls. The number of calls appears to have increased after I made contact and explained that I only have a very small amount of disposable income as I am on Job Seekers Allowance.

STATEMENT OF TRUTH

I believe the facts in this witness statement are true.

Name   Dated:

    Christopher Jones

IN THE NEWTOWN COUNTY COURT   Case No:
B E T W E E N:

MR CHRISTOPHER JONES   Claimant

-and-

BIG UK BANK PLC   Defendant

DRAFT INTERIM ORDER

PENAL NOTICE

IF BIG UK BANK PLC DISOBEY THIS ORDER YOU MAY BE HELD IN CONTEMPT OF COURT AND MAY BE IMPRISONED, FINED OR HAVE YOUR ASSETS SEIZED.

ANY OTHER PERSON WHO KNOWS OF THIS ORDER AND DOES ANYTHING WHICH HELPS OR PERMITS THIS DEFENDANT TO BREACH THE TERMS OF THIS ORDER MAY ALSO BE HELD TO BE IN CONTEMPT OF COURT AND MAY BE IMPRISONED, FINED OR HAVE HIS ASSETS SEIZED

ON HEARING the Claimant in person
AND ON HEARING solicitor the Defendant
AND ON READING the written evidence filed

1.   The Defendant and/or its agents, employees or any person or company instructed on behalf of the Defendant be restrained until the conclusion of the trial of this action or further order from contacting the Claimant in respect of any debts due to them.

2.   The Defendant do pay the Claimants costs of this application summarily assessed at £................

SUMMARY

Court action should be regarded as the last resort and alternatives should be considered. However, if the course of conduct on the part of the creditor or their debt collector has crossed the line into harassment and nothing appears to stop the constant contact, then taking legal action to seek an injunction and damages is the next option. Before commencing legal action, an appropriate "Letter of Claim" should be sent in keeping with pre-action protocol. It is advisable to take proper legal advice before embarking on court action and it may well be that you should engage the services of a lawyer to handle a case of this nature; one thing that you can be sure of is that if you are up against a large organisation they will certainly have resources to respond to your claim and so having a lawyer instructed, who is knowledgeable, in these types of claims would probably be beneficial. This book sets out the important aspects when taking legal action but it is impossible to predict the course a particular case will follow and what legal issues it will throw up.

Chapter 6

What Remedies Can the Court Award For Harassment?

If you are claiming harassment under the Protection from Harassment Act 1997, you can seek an injunction to stop the conduct complained of as well as damages and compensation for the anxiety and stress you have suffered. Where you have commenced proceedings against a creditor for harassment it is likely that an injunction to stop the unreasonable debt collection activities will be granted. You may attempt to seek an interim injunction prior to the full trial of the case if it proceeds that far. If you achieve an interim injunction then that might persuade the defendant to settle the matter at that stage as the interim injunction is in some cases a good indication of how case would be decided at the full hearing.

It should be recognised that an injunction would not be granted on terms that would stop the creditor from taking legal action to pursue the debt they believe is outstanding. What an injunction could stop is the debt collection activity except for the actual bringing of legal proceedings. A court is not going to remove a party's right to take legal proceedings to recover a debt (unless of course the party is the subject to a restraint order arising from them being declared a vexatious litigant).

To claim damages for anxiety and stress the 1997 Act does not require medical evidence of a psychological injury but if there was evidence of such injury then that could be reflected in the damages awarded. Therefore, if you have suffered clinical depression, for example, as result of the harassment, then having medical evidence would have an impact on the level of damages awarded..

As to how a court assesses damages for harassment claimed under the 1997 Act, the case of **S and D Property Investments Ltd v Christian Nisbet and Stephen French (2009)** stated that the calculation of damages for anxiety in harassment cases should not be based on the way damages for injury to feelings is calculated in discrimination cases because damages for anxiety in harassment cases are based on a course of conduct.

However, the way courts now assess damages for anxiety in harassment cases is based on the guidelines in the case of **Vento v Chief Constable of West Yorkshire Police [2002] EWCA Civ 1871**, which gave guidance for assessing damages for injury to feelings. In the case of **Vento**, a probationary police officer; she was the victim of harassment and discrimination by other police officers. She was subsequently dismissed. The applicant brought proceedings in the Employment Tribunal and recovered damages under a number of heads. Within the Judgment in the **Vento** case, there is a paragraph that gave guidance in relation to the assessment of damages for injury to feelings.

65. Employment Tribunals and those who practise in them might find it helpful if this Court were to identify three broad bands of compensation for injury to feelings, as distinct from compensation for psychiatric or similar personal injury. (i) The top band should normally be between £15,000 and £25,000. Sums in this range should be awarded in the most serious cases, such as where there has been a lengthy campaign of discriminatory harassment on the ground of sex or race. This case falls within that band. Only in the most exceptional case should an award of compensation for injury to feelings exceed £25,000. (ii) The middle band of between £5,000 and £15,000 should be used for serious cases, which do not merit an award in the highest band. (iii) Awards of between £500 and £5,000 are appropriate for less serious cases, such as where the act of discrimination is an isolated or one off occurrence. In general, awards of less than £500 are to be avoided altogether, as they risk being regarded as so low as not to be a proper recognition of injury to feelings."

In a more recent case of **Da'Bell v NSPCC [2010] IRLR 19**, the figures determined in the Vento case were increased to allow for inflation and so the top bracket became £18,000 to £30,000, the second bracket £6,000 to £18,000 and the third bracket £600 to £6,000.

The case of **Roberts v Bank of Scotland (2013)** which was considered earlier when looking at what amounts to harassment, used the guidance in Vento to assess damages. In that case, the bank had made no less than 547 calls or attempted calls to Ms Roberts over the period December 2007 to January 2009. The great majority of those calls were made during the first half of 2008. The court awarded her damages.

What is apparent from the damages awarded in **Roberts** is that you cannot expect to receive a pot of gold. If the claimant has suffered a psychological injury then damages could reflect such an injury and damages for injury to feelings, but the court will avoid double recovery. To come within the second bracket (£6,000 to £18,000) of **Vento** for damages for harassment, the amount of contact would need to be pretty high and sustained as experienced by Ms Roberts.

In the case of **Poncelet v Npower (2010)**, Mr Poncelet was awarded £3,000 in damages. Judge Bray described Npower's actions as 'the oppressive and unacceptable conduct of a large company over a small individual'. Mr Poncelet works at night for a US company and so had signed up to an Npower tariff that was cheaper at night. According to Mr Poncelet's solicitors, Npower switched the day and night units as it assumed the readings were wrong. Mr Poncelet had been in dispute with Npower for three years and during that time he received 15 inaccurate bills, telephone calls and 14 visits from debt collectors. Npower were in breach of the OFT guidelines by continuing debt collection activity and ignoring his claims that he did not owe the debt. Judge Bray described Npower's actions as 'the oppressive and unacceptable conduct of a large company over a small individual'. The full Judgment in that case is in Appendix 2 at the end of this book. It is interesting to note that in Poncelet v Npower, the Judge found it a difficult thing to assess damages in respect of harassment at the

93

hands of debt collectors. He took assistance from the guidelines in personal injury cases for damages awarded for stress to come up with a figure, for general damages, totalling £3,000.

In case of **Osborn v Npower (2012)**[14], which was a small claims hearing heard at Bristol County Court, Mr Osborn was awarded £1,000 compensation for harassment. Whilst this was a small claims track case and so not binding, the outcome can still be referred to and might be persuasive when dealing with similar claims. In June 2008, a doorstep salesman working for Npower called the claimant's home offering him a two and half year fixed term contract. Mr Osborn found that tariffs attractive and said he would take out the package provided he could settle bills by online banking/BACS rather than direct debit. The salesman agreed and Mr Osborn signed the contract authorising transfer of his account from his current provider. Within the 14 day cooling-off period Mr Osborn wrote to the Npower confirming the tariffs that had been offered and accepted together with the agreed method of payment. He told them that they must not switch his supply unless they were prepared to honour these terms.

Npower received the letter but did not reply. They switched his supply but set up the account on the standard tariffs. Mr Osborn calculated that this would cost about £2,000 more over the fixed term. He offered to pay by direct debit but was told that the package had been withdrawn. He raised a complaint with Npower; they confirmed that they had mis-sold and awarded him £75 in compensation but continued to bill him at the standard tariff. He informed Npower that the doorstep contract was legally binding and he would hold them to it for the fixed term. He regularly read his meters calculated the bills at the doorstep rates and paid via BACS. By the end of the fixed term his account went into debit. In February 2009, Npower started debt collection proceedings. Mr Osborn sought a decision of the Energy Ombudsman as to whether the "doorstep contract" was binding on Npower. The Ombudsman

---

[14] CILEx Journal March 2013

said that it was not within its powers to determine if there was a breach and Mr Osborn would need to take the matter to court.

Npower aggressively pursued Mr Osborn for the debt. Between 2009 and 20012, he received 56 letters from 10 debt collection agencies, together with numerous telephone calls. He was threatened with disconnection of electricity and gas supplies, warrants of entry from the magistrates courts, forcible entry into his home and visits by doorstep collection agents. Mr Osborn repeatedly wrote to Npower stating this was harassment and asked them to stop, pending the court's decision. Npower ignored him and continued regardless. The Judge ruled that the "doorstep contract" was binding and that the defendant may not rely upon any different or other alleged contract, effectively meaning there was no alleged debt. In addition, the judge said that Npower had no entitlement to send the threatening letters and they had caused distress and anxiety to Mr Osborn and his family. To make such threats without any intention of carrying them out was harassment. Npower was ordered to pay £1,000 compensation for harassment, £200 in what was contractually owed and £500 in costs.

SUMMARY

Under the Protection from Harassment Act 1997, you have a civil remedy. You can obtain an injunction to stop the harassment as well as seeking damages. To be able to claim damages, for anxiety and distress you do not have to show medical evidence that you suffered a mental illness. Obviously evidence of a mental illness, such as depression, would increase the likely damages. In assessing damages for harassment under the 1997 Act, the court will often refer to the guidelines in the case of **Vento** which sets out parameters in respect of damages for injury to feelings arising from harassment. The level of compensation in claims for harassment against debt collectors will depend on the circumstances but, unless the course of conduct is very prolonged and severe, the figure will probably be within the first realm of **Vento**.

Chapter 7

What Will Stop the Merry-Go-Round?

With a more efficient and effective County Court system the temptation is to use bullying tactics would diminish. A properly resourced and efficient court system would go a long way towards restoring faith in its ability to protect those who need to be protected but order those you can and should pay to do so. Also it might actually mean that there will be greater prospects of collecting the money awarded by the court. Such confidence in the system may reduce the need to engage in unfair practice or harassment of debtors. This is hardly a difficult concept and, therefore, one wonders why this has not been addressed. The answer is probably that the government does not have the cash, or does not want to spend the cash, to provide the civil courts with adequate resources. What we have now is a more expensive system consisting of higher court fees to raise revenue it needs because of the policy of making the civil courts self financing. The reality is that the County Court simply does not have sufficient judges and administrative staff to cope with the workload.

Since the reforms of Lord Woolf in 1999, the civil procedure rules have encouraged parties to regard court action as the last resort. It was a sensible aim to encourage cases to be resolved by alternative methods where appropriate but we now have a system where the government has placed much more pressure on litigants to use ADR (predominantly mediation); we have a situation, described by Professor Genn, as the "sound of one hand clapping". By this, Professor Genn meant that, by forcing parties to mediate and neglecting the resourcing of court litigation, there is no effective weapon to be used if mediation is not successful. In the context of debt collection, frustrated creditors have become totally disillusioned with a system that does not enable them to effectively collect what they are owed. It is understandable that where the

County Court system is a byword for delays the creditor will have lost all confidence in recovering debts through the court system and has resorted to practices that sometimes cross the line into harassment. This is by no means an excuse for engaging in unfair tactics but a court process that has no teeth when it comes to enforcing a legitimate judgment is pushing some organisations into ignoring the court process and using more questionable tactics.

The government's response to attempt a more efficient and cost-effective civil justice system is to move towards more centralisation. One such example is the creation of the County Court money claims centre opened in March 2013 in Salford. All money claims are issued either using money claims online or sending papers to the new business centre at Salford. From April 2014, all of the County Courts became one and so each local court is referred to as a hearing centre. One of the problems with a centralised administrative process is that it is more difficult to contact the service if you have an issue with a particular claim. It is notoriously difficult to contact, by telephone, either the County Court Money Claims Centre or Money Claims Online (MCOL). Not only does it appear to be particularly difficult to contact local county court hearing centres, where a claim is transferred to one when it becomes defended, you often cannot speak directly to the court office but instead you get put through to a call centre. Many County Courts are having restricted opening times for their counters and some courts are even resorting to an appointment system to attend the counter if you have an urgent matter. In addition, it is taking local hearing centres a long time to list even the most straightforward of small claims. In many cases, you will have to wait six months or more for a case to be heard. The changes to the opening hours of court counters might seem a way of allowing the court staff to get on with the paperwork without interruption, but the reality is that it is a cover for the fact that there is a significant shortage of administrative staff.

To speed up the court administration would also require the use of more deputy district judges to deal with the "box work" instead of waiting for the sitting district judges to fit in the

97

paperwork around the hearings. "Box work" includes the various paper applications, allocation questionnaires and other paperwork that a District Judge will have to work through in addition to conducting the hearings. Having more deputy district judges allocated to doing box work may weed out more claims and defences that have no merit.

Not all improvements to the civil court system require a large injection of funding. There are a number of changes, both administratively and procedurally, that would make better use of the limited resources. From a procedural point of view, the court rules have grown since the Woolf Reforms of 1999 like an unkempt Leylandii hedge. Too many case management requirements and new additions to the Civil Procedure Rules have created wasteful and time consuming "spin-off" litigation to decide what the rules mean.

Small businesses, want a decision to be made in cases where a customer is disputing a bill. They don't want to line the pockets of mediators, or lawyers for that matter; they want a swift decision to be made and to get paid, which will keep their businesses afloat. They see the problem with the current system as being a process that is frustratingly slow and heavily in favour of those who do not want to pay. In many ways, the Woolf reforms tackled the problem the wrong way around. To the layperson, they would have liked the enforcement process to have been reformed first and to have been given teeth which it still does not have. The problem with those in charge of running the court system is they don't listen to the ordinary person and seem to have little knowledge of the real world. There are "consultations" but this, in many eyes, is a euphemism for a something that is going to happen anyway but must go through the motions before it occurs.

So what is my answer to the crisis in the court system? Certainly not more pressure to mediate. However, I am realistic enough to know that politicians are not going to find the money needed to properly resource the courts. However, not all changes will require additional funding. What is needed is a bit of imagination when it comes to administering the courts and a greater use of other forms of ADR, namely arbitration and adjudication, and not simply mediation.

We need more district judges in the County Court and the use of more deputies to assist with box work. Perhaps appointing a new class of deputy district judges who simply handle box work would help. In commercial situations, where the parties are represented, and in order to free up court time, it could be left to the parties to provide a venue for the hearing. So the parties to a commercial dispute would hire the judge from a list of those available which would be provided by the court. Also, perhaps there can be greater use of telephone hearings, even for hearings where final decisions are made, such as small claims. Many county court lists are filled up with small claims that are listed for an hour or 90 minutes when in reality many of these claims could be decided by an interventionist judge during a 30 minute telephone hearing.

The litigation process should to be simplified to reduce costs. We should extend the modified procedure of the "small claims track" to larger claims and remove all pointless and time wasting case management in the other tracks. Remove the time spent completing cost budgets and introduce fixed costs to the fast and multi tracks so that the parties will know from the beginning what they can recover; if a party wants to spend more then that is up to them. We could also do away with time consuming disclosure. As in the small claims track, let the parties provide the documents they wish to rely on at trial. There is talk about parties bringing unnecessary litigation; well, surely, all the time spent case managing is not a great use of judicial resources, is it? If much of the procedural burden is cut back then the court might cope with issuing court claims and if the case is defended then it could assign a judge to decide the dispute and leave it to the parties, where appropriate, to set up the hearing. Woolf was all about simplifying procedure and reducing costs but in recent times there has been too much emphasis on case management.

This greatly slimmed down procedure might seem rather like a "Judge Judy" styled system but, in my view, it would be better than no civil justice, which is what we are in danger of moving towards

99

because of the obsession with mediation. If there is better access to justice, then there is the prospect that the merry-go-round will stop spinning.

SUMMARY

In the real world, there will always be choices that have to be made and no bottomless pit of money. However, the imbalance with regard to the resources and attention given to the civil court system, as opposed to the alternatives, has created a serious problem in this country with organisations and individuals believing that those who owe money can simply get away with not paying a debt. The perceived collapsing of the county courts has led, to a large degree, towards the process which has been described in this book as the debt collecting merry-go-round. It is all very well regulating debt collectors but if there is no effective court system then it is understandable that there has been a drift towards tactics which attempt to extract payment by means that may not always be fair and sometimes cross the line into harassment.

Appendix 1

1. Part 8 Claim Form: N208

2. Court fee remission form

3. Acknowledgment of Service Form

Claim Form
(CPR Part 8)

SEAL

Claimant

Mr Christopher Jones
10 Canal Road
Newtown
NN1 2ES

Defendant(s)

Big UK Bank Plc
Head Office
Newtown
NN1 3RT

Does your claim include any issues under the Human Rights Act 1998? ☐ Yes ☑ No

Details of claim *(see also overleaf)*

1. I am a Quantity Surveyor by profession. I borrowed £12,000 from the Defendant. I had not been behind with any repayments until I lost my job when I was made redundant. I had £8,000 outstanding on the loan. I wrote to the Defendant on xx/xx/xx, following a call from the Defendant on xx/xx/xx, setting out my financial circumstances in full. I provided an income and expenditure statement following assistance from the Citizens Advice Bureau. I received the response dated xx/xx/xx which is attached and marked CJ1. I then wrote a further detailed letter dated xx/xx/xx in which I make clear that the constant telephone calls were causing me distress. This letter is attached and marked CJ2.

2. The Defendant's response of xx/xx/xx, stated that "although I am aware you have no funds available to offer, we are unable to hold off taking action on your account until an acceptable offer is made". A copy of this letter is attached and marked CJ3. I received further correspondence and calls and they stated that until an acceptable payment plan is agreed collection activities would continue. I responded to the first of these letters by saying that if they did not accept the situation, they had the right to take court action against me. I attach this correspondence marked CJ4.

Defendant's name and address	Big UK Bank Plc Head Office Newtown NN1 3RT		£
		Court fee	280.00
		Legal representative's costs	
		Issue date	

For further details of the courts www.gov.uk/find-court-tribunal.
When corresponding with the Court, please address forms or letters to the Manager and always quote the claim number.

N208 Claim form (CPR Part 8) (05.14) © Crown copyright 20

Claim no.	

Details of claim *(continued)*

3. I also attach to this Claim Form a sheet marked CJ5 detailing the dates of the telephone calls and texts which I received from the Defendant (or those acting on behalf of the Defendant) in the three month period from xx/xx/xx to yy/yy/yy. There were considerable number of calls and as can be seen on some days I received 5 calls. The number of calls increased after I had detailed my financial position.

4. I claim that the conduct of the Defendant amounts to harassment under section 1 of the Protection from Harassment Act 1997 (the "Act"). I claim damages under section 3 of the Act and an injunction to restrain the Defendant from harassing me. I also seek the costs of making this claim.

5. Under CPR Part 65.28 (1) (a) the Claim shall be subject to the Part 8 procedure.

Statement of Truth

*(I believe)(The Claimant believes) that the facts stated in these particulars of claim are true.
* I am duly authorised by the claimant to sign this statement.

Full name ___CHRISTOPHER JONES_____

Name of claimant's legal representative's firm _____

signed _____*C Jones*_____   position or office held_____
    *(Claimant)(Litigation friend)   (if signing on behalf of firm or company)
    (Legal representative's solicitor)

delete as appropriate

Claimant's or claimant's legal representative's address to which documents should be sent if different from overleaf. If you are prepared to accept service by DX, fax or e-mail, please add details.

Application for a fee remission

Ref. no.
(staff use only)

Protect
Personal Data — EX160

Please read the EX160A booklet 'Court and Tribunal fees — Do I have to pay them? Failure to provide the correct evidence will result in your application being refused. Please complete this form in **CAPITAL LETTERS**

1. About the case

Case, claim or notice to pay number
(leave blank if this is a new case/claim)

What is the title or number of the form to which your fee remission relates?

Name of claimant(s)/ petitioner(s)/applicant(s)

Name of defendant(s)/ respondent(s)

If applicable, give the address of the property to which the dispute relates

For Probate cases only

Name of deceased

Date of death

2. Your details

Title (preferred)   ☐ Mr   ☐ Mrs   ☐ Miss   ☐ Ms   ☐ Other

Surname/family name

First and middle names

Date of birth

Telephone number   Email

Your address

Postcode

What is your status?

Please read page 7 of the EX160A booklet for further guidance on contrary interest.

☐ Single person   ☐ Part of a couple

☐ Part of a couple — **but applying for proceedings with a contrary interest**   **What is the contrary interest?**

Do you have any children?   ☐ Yes   ☐ No   If Yes, how many are financially dependent on you?

3. For Court of Protection cases only (Please read page 8 of the EX160A booklet for further guidance on how to complete this section)

Does your application relate to   ☐ Property and financial affairs   ☐ Health and personal welfare   ☐ Both

Are you applying for remission based on your (the applicant's) circumstances or the person the application is about?

☐ Remission based on the person's circumstances

☐ Remission based on the applicant's circumstances   **Are you the partner of the person?**   ☐ Yes ☐ No

4. Disposable capital test   (This section must be completed before moving to section 5, please read page 9 of the EX160A booklet for further guidance)

Fee to be paid   £

Disposable capital threshold for this fee   £

Is your partner 61 or over?
(if applicable)   ☐ Yes   ☐ No

Is your disposable capital below the threshold you have entered in the box above?   ☐ Yes   ☐ No

If Yes, Go to section 5

If No, you are not eligible for a fee remission. Do not continue with this application unless you believe you have exceptional circumstances.

Remission 1 — full remission based on permitted benefits or Scottish Civil Legal Aid granted for the proceedings to which this fee remission application relates (in the Employment Tribunal and Employment Appeal Tribunal only).

Do you receive any of these benefits

You must provide correctly dated documentary evidence to show you receive one of these benefits.

Please read page 12–13 of the EX160A booklet for further guidance on how to complete this section.

☐ Income-based Jobseeker's Allowance

☐ Universal Credit — with gross annual earnings of less than £6,000

☐ None of the above — **Go to section 6**

☐ Income-related Employment and Support Allowance

☐ State Pension — Guarantee Credit

☐ Income Support

Scottish Civil Legal Aid (**not** Advice and Assistance or Advice by way of Representation)

If you have ticked any of the above boxes **Go to Section 7**

Remission 2 — full or part remission based on gross monthly income

What is your gross monthly income?

Gross monthly income is your total monthly income before tax and other deductions.

Excluded benefits are listed on page 17 of the EX160A booklet.

You must provide correctly dated documentary evidence of your income.

Please read page 14–15 of the EX160A booklet for further guisance on how to complete this section.

	Applicant	Partner
Paid/Self employment	£	£
Money from anyone living with you — lodger/tenant, relative etc.	£	£
Total pensions — state, private, occupational	£	£
Child benefit	£	£
Other benefit — do not include excluded benefits	£	£
Income from rents, shares, bonds, or other financial arrangement	£	£
Any other income	£	£
Total gross monthly income	£ 0.00	£ 0.00

Refund

Are you applying for a refund of court/tribunal/probate fee paid within the last three months, or a Court of Protection fee paid in the last three months from the date of a Final Order?

☐ Yes ☐ No If Yes, what is the date you paid this fee, or what is the date of the Court of Protection Final Order?

Declaration and statement of truth

Please ensure that you provide the evidence required to support your application as set out in the EX160A booklet.

I believe that the facts and information stated in this application are true. I understand that if you tell anything untrue in this form, or the accompanying documents, leave anything out or fail to provide sufficient evidence:

- •.. My application may be refused and the full fee will be payable
- •.. Any order or process obtained as a result of this application can be revoked
- •.. If I am found to have been deliberately untruthful, criminal proceedings may be brought against me for fraud.

☐ I have attached the evidence needed to support my application

Signature _____ Date _____

Full name _____

Once you have completed this form, please submit it, with the correct evidence, to the court, tribunal or probate office

For the court/probate/tribunal office use only

		Risk controls
Name of court, tribunal or probate office	Threshold for fee correct ☐ Yes ☐ No	Signature
Reference no.	Evidence for remission ☐ 1 ☐ 2	
Form no.	Fee charge applicable £	Name
Signature	Amount remitted £	
Name	Amount to pay £	Band Date
Band Date	Date approved	

Acknowledgment of Service
(Part 8 claim)

In the	
Claim No.	
Claimant (including ref)	
Defendant	

You should read the 'notes for defendant' attached to the claim form which will tell you how to complete this form, and when and where to send it.

Tick and complete sections A - E as appropriate.
In all cases you must complete sections F and G

Section A

☐ I **do not** intend to contest this claim

Give details of any order, direction, etc. you are seeking from the court.

Section B

☐ I intend to contest this claim

Give brief details of any different remedy you are seeking.

Section C

☐ I intend to dispute the court's jurisdiction
(Please note, any application must be filed within 14 days of the date on which you file this acknowledgment of service)

The court office at

is open between 10 am and 4 pm Monday to Friday. When corresponding with the court, please address forms or letters to the Court Manager and quote the claim number.
N210 Acknowledgment of Service (CPR Part 8) (3.01)   *Printed on behalf of The Court Service*

Section D

☐ I object to the claimant issuing under this procedure

My reasons for objecting are:

Section E

☐ I intend to rely on written evidence

My written evidence:

☐ is filed with this form

☐ will be filed within 14 days as agreed with the other party(ies). A copy of the written agreement is attached to this form

Section F

Full name of defendant filing
this acknowledgment _____

Section G

| **Signed**
(To be signed by you or by your solicitor or litigation friend) | *(I believe)(The defendant believes) that the facts stated in this form are true. *I am duly authorised by the defendant to sign this statement

*delete as appropriate | **Position or office held**
(if signing on behalf of firm or company) | |

Date [   ]

Give an address to which notices about this case can be sent to you			if applicable	
		Ref. no.	
		fax no.	
	Postcode	DX no.	
	Tel. no.	e-mail	

Appendix 2

Cases:

1. Roberts v Bank of Scotland (2013)

2. Ferguson v. British Gas Trading Ltd (2009)

3. Poncelet v. NPower Ltd (2010)

4. S&D Property Investments Ltd v. Nisbet & French (2009)

Neutral Citation Number: [2013] EWCA Civ 882
IN THE COURT OF APPEAL (CIVIL DIVISION)
ON APPEAL FROM DEWSBURY COUNTY COURT
(HIS HONOUR JUDGE SHAUN SPENCER QC)

Royal Courts of Justice
Strand
London WC2A 2LL

Date: Tuesday, 11 June 2013

B e f o r e:

LADY JUSTICE ARDEN
LORD JUSTICE JACKSON
and
LORD JUSTICE McCOMBE

- -

Between:

ROBERTS

Claimant/Respondent

and

BANK OF SCOTLAND PLC

Defendant/Appellant

- -

(DAR Transcript of
WordWave International Limited
A Merrill Communications Company
165 Fleet Street, London EC4A 2DY
Tel No: 020 7404 1400   Fax No: 020 7831 8838
Official Shorthand Writers to the Court)

- -

Mr James Counsell (instructed by DLA Piper UK LLP) appeared on behalf of the **Appellant**.

The **Respondent** appeared in person.

- -

JUDGMENT

LORD JUSTICE JACKSON:
1.   This judgment is in seven parts, namely:
Part 1. Introduction.
Part 2. The facts,
Part 3. The present proceedings,
Part 4. The appeal to the Court of Appeal,
Part 5. Liability,
Part 6. Quantum of damages,
Part 7. Conclusion.

Part 1.   Introduction

2.   This is an appeal by a bank which has been ordered to pay £7,500 damages to a customer whom it harassed by repeated telephone calls.   The bank disputes both liability and quantum.

3.   The claimant in this action and respondent in the Court of Appeal is Miss Amanda Roberts.   The claimant is a 48-year_old lady who lives in Dewsbury.

4.   The defendant in the action and appellant in the Court of Appeal is Bank of Scotland Plc.   The defendant has taken over the business of Halifax Plc and that business now forms one division of Bank of Scotland.   The entity with which the claimant dealt at all material times operated under the name "Halifax".   I shall therefore refer to the defendant as "Halifax" or "the bank".

5.   I shall refer to the Protection from Harassment Act 1997 as "the 1997 Act".   Section 1(1) of the 1997 Act provides:

"1. (1) A person must not pursue a course of conduct-

(a) which amounts to harassment of another, and

(b) which he knows or ought to know amounts to harassment of the other."

6.   Section 2 of the 1997 Act provides:

"(1) A person who pursues a course of conduct in breach of section 1 (1) or (1A) is guilty of an offence.

(2) A person guilty of an offence under this section is liable on summary conviction to imprisonment for a term not exceeding six months, or a fine not exceeding level 5 on the standard scale, or both."

7.   Section 3 of the 1997 Act provides:

"(1) An actual or apprehended breach of section 1 (1) may be the subject of a claim in civil proceedings by the person who is or may be the victim of the course of conduct in question.

(2) On such a claim, damages may be awarded for (among other things) any anxiety caused by the harassment and any financial loss resulting from the harassment."

8.   Section 7 of the 1997 Act provides:

"(2) References to harassing a person include alarming the person or causing the person distress.

(3) A "course of conduct" must involve-

(a) in the case of conduct in relation to a single person (see section 1(1)), conduct on at least two occasions in relation to that person, or

(b) in the case of conduct in relation to two or more persons (see section 1(1A)), conduct on at least one occasion in relation to each of those persons."

9.   After these introductory remarks, I must now turn to the facts.

10.   During 2007 and 2008 the claimant was a customer of Halifax.   Her account was held at the Leeds office of the Halifax, but the branch which she regularly used was at Dewsbury.   The claimant had three accounts with Halifax. There was a current account, a credit card account and a loan account.   The current account had an overdraft limit of £1,250.   The credit card account had a credit limit of £2,700.   The loan account comprised a loan of £7,350, repayable in 86 monthly instalments commencing in April 2006.

11.   There were periods when the claimant exceeded her overdraft limit on the current account or exceeded the credit limit on her credit card account.   On the basis of the figures which counsel has mentioned in argument today, it appears that the amounts by which the claimant exceeded her limits were modest.

12.   With a view to resolving these matters, the bank decided to contact the claimant by telephone.   There is nothing objectionable in taking that course.   The problem in this case lies in the sheer number of phone calls that were made and the content of those calls. According to the bank's log, bank staff made no less than 547 calls or attempted calls to the claimant over the period December 2007 to January 2009.   The great majority of those calls were made during the first half of 2008.

13.   The claimant made it perfectly plain to bank staff during these calls that she did not wish to talk to them and she wanted them to stop telephoning.   The bank staff refused to desist.   They insisted that they would go on telephoning until the claimant answered their security questions and discussed her financial position with them.

14.   The claimant tape recorded some of these telephone calls.   Transcripts of the recorded calls have been prepared and they make remarkable reading.   The callers are a variety of different people, who ring from call centres dotted around Britain and Ireland.   One caller callously talks about the bank ringing the claimant a hundred times or so.

15.   The claimant was greatly distressed by the bombardment of phone calls from the bank.   She took the view that this conduct amounted to harassment.   Accordingly, she commenced the present proceedings.

Part 3.   The present proceedings

16.   By a claim form issued in the Dewsbury County Court on 27 April 2010, the claimant claimed damages for the harassment perpetrated by Halifax.   On 13 August 2010, the claimant served her particulars of claim.

17.   The claimant has at all times acted as a litigant in person.   Nevertheless, her pleadings are clear and to the point. Paragraph 12 of the particulars of claim gives a fair indication of her case.   This reads as follows:

> "From 28th December 2007 the defendant has embarked on a sustained campaign of harassment directed towards the claimant.   The unacceptable course of conduct began with telephone calls to her and to her parents.   It is believed that the reason for this course conduct was in pursuit of an alleged debt/s.   The claimant will show that her current account was funded and not outside of its agreed limits from January 8th 2008 until May 8th 2008 and that further defaults to other accounts were caused by the defendant.   Furthermore, the defendant knew or should have known that their course of conduct was causing harm and was unlikely to resolve the situation.
>
> On or around 24th December 2007 and again on 3rd January 2008 and again on 14 January 2008 letters were posted to the claimant at her parents address.   (As detailed above in Data Particulars)
>
> On January 9th 2008 the defendant attempted to contact the claimant eight times in a twelve hour period.   Five of these calls were answered two of these by the claimant and three by her parents. The claimant avers that this communication was oppressive and unacceptable and that she was particularly aggrieved by it."

18.   After various interlocutory skirmishes, the details of which are not relevant, the bank served a defence and counter_claim on 29 November 2011.   In its defence the bank admitted making a large number of phone calls to the claimant, but denied that these amounted to harassment.   The bank averred that these were reasonable attempts to contact its customer.   The bank also counterclaimed for outstanding sums due on the three accounts.   These amounted to £10,941.37 plus interest.

19.   The action came on for trial before HHJ Shaun Spencer QC at the Bradford County Court in February 2012.   The

claimant duly presented her case and gave evidence. Mr James Counsell, instructed by DLA Piper UK LLP, represented the bank. The judge delivered his reserved judgment on 10 February 2012. He concluded that the bank's phone calls did indeed constitute harassment. He awarded damages to be assessed. The judge also gave judgment in favour of the defendant for the sum claimed in the counterclaim. There has been no dispute about the counterclaim.

20. The hearing to assess damages took place at Bradford County Court on 27 September 2012. The judge assessed the bank's liability for damages in the sum of £7,500. I would briefly summarise the judge's reasoning in relation to quantum as follows. The judge concluded that some of the calls were intimidatory and that those calls must be viewed in the context of the totality of the calls, which were very frequent and on most days of the week. The judge regarded the claimant as a genuine witness. He noted her distress when the recordings of certain calls were played in court. He regarded that distress as genuine. The judge had regard to the authorities on quantum to which I shall refer a little later, and he concluded that the proper measure of damages was £7,500.

21. The bank was aggrieved by the judge's decisions, both on liability and quantum. Accordingly, the bank has appealed to the Court of Appeal.

Part 4. The appeal to the Court of Appeal

22. By an appellant's notice dated 17 October 2012, the bank appealed against the judge's decisions on liability and quantum. In relation to liability, I would summarise the grounds of appeal set out in the appellant's notice as follows:
(1) The judge failed to take into account the context in which the calls were made, in particular the fact that the bank had good reason to telephone the claimant.
(2) The staff who rang the claimant were civil and polite.
(3) The judge was selective in the extracts from phone call transcripts which he cited in his judgment.
(4) The judge failed to apply the guidance in the authorities.
(5) The judge failed to address the question of whether the bank knew or ought to have known that its conduct amounted to harassment.

23. In relation to quantum of damages, the grounds of appeal relate the circumstances of the case at some length and then contend that the award of £7,500 was excessive and outside the margin of judicial discretion.

24. At the hearing of this appeal today, Mr Counsell appears for the bank, as he did in the court below. As before, the claimant, who is now respondent, appears in person.

25. Mr Counsell may possibly have detected in the course of his submissions that the court was not entirely sympathetic to this appeal. Despite that circumstance, Mr Counsell presented the bank's case courteously, fairly and fully. I am grateful to him for his assistance.

26. The claimant is also here, no doubt fully prepared to argue her case. In the event, we did not need to call upon her. The claimant readily accepted that in those circumstances she did not need to say anything in relation to the bank's appeal.

27. Having set the scene, I must now turn to the bank's appeal on liability.

Part 5. Liability

28. In their daily lives most people regularly interact with friends, colleagues, opponents, acquaintances and strangers. Inevitably not all of these interactions are harmonious. Some cause annoyance and irritation, on occasions considerable annoyance and irritation. These inevitable turbulences of daily life have nothing at all to do with the crime of harassment. In the context of the 1997 Act, "harassment" is both a crime and a civil wrong. It connotes deliberate conduct directed against other people which attains a certain level of severity. Three recent authorities give guidance on the gravity of the conduct which is required to constitute harassment.

29. In Majrowski v Guy's and Thomas's NHS Trust [2006] UKHL 34; [2007] 1 AC 224, a clerical worker claimed damages for harassment by his departmental manager. Both the Court of Appeal and the House of Lords held that an employer could be vicariously liable for harassment by its manager and accordingly the claim should not be struck out. In relation to what constitutes harassment, Lord Nicholls said this at paragraph 30:

> "... courts will have in mind that irritations, annoyances, even a measure of upset, arise at times in everybody's day_to_day dealings with other people. Courts are well able to recognise the boundary between conduct which is unattractive, even unreasonable, and conduct which is

oppressive and unacceptable. To cross the boundary from the regrettable to the unacceptable the gravity of the misconduct must be of an order which would sustain criminal liability under section 2."

30.   Baroness Hale observed that the aim of the 1997 Act was the prevention of harassment in all its forms. At paragraph 66, she continued:

> "If this was the aim, it is easy to see why the definition of harassment was left deliberately wide and open_ended. It does require a course of conduct, but this can be shown by conduct on at least two occasions (or since 2005 by conduct on one occasion to each of two or more people): section 7(3). All sorts of conduct may amount to harassment. It includes alarming a person or causing her distress: section 7(2). But conduct might be harassment even if no alarm or distress were in fact caused. A great deal is left to the wisdom of the courts to draw sensible lines between the ordinary banter and badinage of life and genuinely offensive and unacceptable behaviour."

31.   In Sunderland City Council v Conn [2007] EWCA Civ 1492; [2008] IRLR 324, a paver employed by the Council alleged harassment by his foreman. Two specific incidents were established on the evidence. In the first incident, the foreman lost his temper. He threatened to smash the windows of the site cabin and to report three men to the personnel department. The claimant was one of those three men. The other two men were not bothered by the foreman's behaviour. In the second incident, the foreman lost his temper again. He threatened to give the claimant "a good hiding" even if that led to the foreman being dismissed.

32.   The Court of Appeal held that the first incident was not serious enough to constitute harassment. The second incident did cross the line, but since more than one incident was required by section 7(3)(a) of the 1997 Act, the claimant's claim failed. Gage LJ emphasised the importance of the context in which the relevant conduct occurs. At paragraph 12, he said:

> "It seems to me that what, in the words of Lord Nicholls in Majrowski, crosses the boundary between unattractive and even unreasonable conduct and conduct which is oppressive and unacceptable, may well depend on the context in which the conduct occurs. What might not be harassment on the factory floor or in the barrack room might well be harassment in the hospital ward and vice versa. In my judgment the touchstone for recognising what is not harassment for the purposes of sections 1 and 3 will be whether the conduct is of such gravity as to justify the sanctions of the criminal law."

33.   In Ferguson v British Gas Trading Limited [2009] EWCA Civ 46; [2010] 1 WLR 785, the defendant supplied gas to the claimant until 25 May 2006. Thereafter, owing to some technical error, the defendant sent a series of computer generated bills and demands to the claimant for sums which she did not owe. Some letters contained threats to disconnect the claimant's gas supply and report her to credit rating agencies. The claimant brought a claim for harassment which both Judge Seymour QC and the Court of Appeal refused to strike out.

34.   Jacob LJ accepted that a course of conduct must be grave if it is to constitute the crime or the tort of harassment. He then added these comments in paragraph 18:

> "In so accepting I would just add this word of caution: the fact of parallel criminal and civil liability is not generally, outside the particular context of harassment, of significance in considering civil liability. There are a number of other civil wrongs which are also crimes. Perhaps most common would be breaches of the Trade Descriptions Act 1968 as amended. In the field of intellectual property both trade mark and copyright infringement, and the common law tort of passing off (which generally involves deception), may all amount to crimes. It has never been suggested generally that the scope of a civil wrong is restricted because it is also a crime. What makes the wrong of harassment different and special is because, as Lord Nicholls and Lady Hale recognised, in life one has to put up with a certain amount of annoyance: things have got to be fairly severe before the law, civil or criminal, will intervene."

35.   Fortified by this guidance from the authorities, let me now turn to the bank's conduct in the present case. The first point to make is that whenever the claimant exceeded her permitted level of indebtedness to the bank, she was in breach of contract. The bank was entitled to pursue its legal rights. The bank could sue the claimant for sums which were owing. If it wished to do so, the bank could withdraw its services from the claimant and leave her to take her

custom elsewhere.

36.   Before taking any of these drastic courses, it obviously made sense for the bank to contact the claimant and to seek a mutually acceptable resolution of the problem.   Possibly the bank could help the claimant through a difficult period. Possibly the bank could set up a new arrangement for repaying the claimant's indebtedness.   This might, for example, involve reduced instalments paid over a longer period.   With these matters in mind, it made perfectly good sense for the bank to write to the claimant and also to telephone her.   Indeed, any creditor should make contact with his debtor to request and discuss repayment before embarking upon formal legal proceedings.

37.   The existence of a debt, however, does not give the creditor the right to bombard the debtor with endless and repeated telephone calls.   The debtor is fully entitled to say that he or she does not wish to talk to the creditor.   In those circumstances, the creditor is thrown back upon his formal legal remedies.   That is what the courts are there to provide. They are there to ensure that creditors do not resort to the remedy of self help.

38.   In the present case, the claimant made it abundantly plain that she did not wish to receive telephone calls from the bank. She was perfectly entitled to adopt this position.   Once the bank had tried to telephone the claimant a few times and had received the same response on each occasion, it was obvious that telephoning the claimant would achieve nothing. Thereafter, there was no possible justification for continuing to ring the claimant up.

39.   The judge took the view that the content of the phone calls made by the bank, combined with the frequency of those calls, constituted harassment.   The bank challenges that conclusion for the reasons which I have summarised in Part 4 above.   I will address those arguments in the order set out in the appellant's notice, bearing in mind the very helpful submissions with which Mr Counsell has elaborated those grounds today.

40.   The first argument is that the judge failed to take into account the context in which the calls were made, in particular the fact that the bank had good reason to telephone the claimant.   Mr Counsell found himself in considerable difficulties when developing this line of argument.   The court, prompted by paragraph 12 of the claimant's particulars of claim, asked Mr Counsell to address the period 8 January 2008 to 11 February 2008 when there was a large number of phone calls and the content was particularly unpleasant.   Mr Counsell explained that during this period the claimant had exceeded the limit on her credit card account.   We asked by how much.   Mr Counsell told us that the limit was £2,700.   On 25 January 2008, the balance on that account was £2,789.   So the claimant was £89 over the limit.   At the end of the relevant period, the balance was £2,717.   So the claimant was £17 over the limit.

41.   During this period, as the judge found and as the appellant now admits, the bank had wrongly frozen the claimant's current account.   A sum of £450 housing benefit was paid into the current account, which the claimant could have accessed if the account had not been frozen.   That was more than enough to pay the small excess on the credit card account.   Indeed, if the account had not been frozen, the bank could, and no doubt would, have transferred funds across from the current account to the credit card account to resolve this matter without the need for any instructions from the claimant.   Mr Counsell confirmed in answer to Arden LJ that the bank had this power.

42.   I therefore take the view that the calls which the bank made during the period 8th January to 12th February 2008 were wholly unwarranted.

43.   Let me now leave that aspect on one side and assume hypothetically that the claimant was to some extent overdrawn on every occasion when a member of staff rang the claimant.   Even so, that context cannot possibly justify the number of calls which the bank made or their content.   The mere fact that the creditor is a bank rather than a private individual does not give a licence to bombard the debtor with unwarranted and unpleasant phone calls.   This court emphasised in the Sunderland case that the context is important.   The context here is a well resourced bank with an automated dialling system and a series of call centres on one hand, contacting a single lady living alone, who appears to be in some financial difficulties.   I do not accept that the judge overlooked any relevant features of the context in this case.

44.   The second line of argument on behalf of the bank is that the staff who rang the claimant were civil and polite.   This was a point Mr Counsell developed this morning.   I do not accept this line of argument.

45.   I shall read out two extracts from the transcripts.   The first extract is to be found on pages 1 and 2 of one of the phone calls made on 8 January 2008.   The claimant made it clear that she wished not to be telephoned again, but the caller refused to comply with this request.   The claimant then said: "I mean, do I have to, do I have to do this, how many times a day are you going to ring me".   The caller replied: "Well until you speak to us and co_operate with us we are going to continue to call you with regards to this matter".   The claimant said "pardon?".   The caller replied: "Until you're willing to speak to us and co_operate with us we will continue to call you -- obviously that's why we need to speak to you urgently".

46.   The second extract which I will read is to be found on pages 1 and 2 of one of the phone calls made on
        10 January 2008:

> "AR   Why am I getting these calls when I keep asking you to stop ringing me?
> Caller   Is this Amanda I'm talking to, yeah?
> AR   Are you deaf?
> Caller   Right, Amanda we won't stop the calls unless we talk to you
> AR   And do you know that I keep asking over and over again for you to not ring me?   And I will contact my bank directly
>   and speak to them
> Caller   Right
> AR   Over and over again I keep asking you and you keep ringing me, I'm getting calls at ten past eight in the morning and
>   ten to ten at night
> Caller   You will do
> AR   I will do?   Over and over again?
> Caller   Yes, do you want me to stop the calls coming out to you?
> AR   Excuse me!   How many times have I asked?
> Caller   Right, so we need to have a quick chat then, OK?   I just need....
> AR   No I don't think so!   Stop ringing me!
> Caller   OK, we'll give you a ring later
> AR   No you won't!
> Caller   Yes we will!
> AR   Oh, and you're just going to keep doing it over and over again?
> Caller   Yes, until you talk to us, OK?
> AR   And that's how you behave as a business is it?
> Caller   What?   Because we want to talk?
> AR   You call it talking?   I call it harassment!
> Caller   How can it be harassment if you're not going to talk to us?   Have you got two minutes?"

47.   Many similar passages can be found in the transcripts.   The judge characterised these calls as intimidatory.   I agree
        with that characterisation.

48.   It is no defence to intimidation that the culprit couched the intimidatory words in polite language, if that is how one
        characterises extracts of the kind which I have just read out.

49.   The third line of argument deployed in the appellant's notice is that the judge was selective in the extracts from the
        phone call transcripts which he cited.   For my part, I would accept that the judge had to make a selection.   It would
        have been impossible for him to set out in a judgment of reasonable length the entirety of the transcripts which have
        been furnished to this court.   Nevertheless, I have read the entirety of those transcripts.   I consider that the extracts
        set out by the judge give a fair flavour of the unacceptable phone calls, and that there are other phone calls similar to
        those from which the judge quoted.   On some occasions the claimant says that the calls are making her ill.   It can be
        seen that the bank staff take no notice.   They say that they will continue telephoning.

50.   The fourth argument on behalf of the bank is that the judge failed to apply the guidance in the authorities.   I do not
        accept this argument.   The judge identified the relevant authorities, including those which I have summarised above.
        He then considered whether the bank's conduct achieved the requisite level of seriousness to constitute harassment
        within the meaning of the 1997 Act.   He concluded that it did.

51.   Mr Counsell valiantly argued that the bank's repeated calls come nowhere near criminal conduct.   I do not agree. I
        bear in mind and agree with the observations of Jacobs LJ in paragraph 18 of <u>Ferguson</u> as quoted above.   In my view,
        the bank's conduct in the present case easily crosses the threshold.   It was harassment which could have been
        prosecuted in the criminal courts.   In the event, and fortunately for the bank, this matter simply comes before the civil
        courts as a claim for damages.

52.   The fifth line of argument set out in the appellant's notice is that the judge failed to address the question of whether the
        bank knew or ought to have known that its conduct amounted to harassment.   This is clearly a relevant matter because
        section 1(1) of the 1997 Act makes it clear that one element of the offence of harassment or the civil wrong of
        harassment is knowledge that what the defendant is doing amounts to harassment of the other person.

53.   Very wisely Mr Counsell did not press this argument to any extent in his oral submissions.   The bank must have been
        perfectly well aware of the phone calls which it was making.   It kept a record of them in its log.   The callers appear
        to have been keeping a record of the gist of the conversations which they had with the claimant.   If they were not
        keeping such a record on occasions, they certainly should have been.

54. I suggested to Mr Counsell during argument that if the bank really wanted a constructive dialogue with the claimant, it may have been sensible for the manager of the Dewsbury branch to telephone the claimant. The manager, unlike the various people in the call centres, knew the claimant, and the claimant had more than once tried to talk to her.

55. Mr Counsell responded that banks like Halifax have large numbers of customers who are overdrawn at any given time. It is quite impracticable for the local manager to ring such people up. Instead, Halifax, like other banks, has a variety of call centres. There is apparently an automated dialling system, whereby a computer rings up defaulting customers. If the customer answers the call, then he or she is routed to any available member of staff at one of the call centres. It is the bank's case that a system like this is the only practicable one.

56. Although Mr Counsell made his submissions attractively, I am unpersuaded. The Dewsbury branch of Halifax will have had a finite number of customers who were seriously in arrears. I would have thought it simpler and cheaper for the local manager to telephone the claimant and try to talk to her, rather than unleash a monstrous system of 547 automated phone calls followed by a series of futile conversations. In these conversations the caller is always someone different. His or her knowledge of the claimant is gleaned from notes on a database.

57. In my view, the bank should amend its system so that it treats customers with courtesy, or at the very least so that it does not commit the crime and tort of harassment. If Mr Counsell is right in saying that the only practicable means by which a bank can contact defaulting customers is the method adopted in this case, then banks had better build into their costings the damages which from time to time they will be called upon to pay to those customers. There is also the matter of criminal penalties to be considered.

58. For the reasons indicated above, I would dismiss the bank's appeal on liability. The only remaining issue, therefore, is in respect of quantum of damages.

Part 6. Quantum of damages

59. In assessing damages, the judge directed himself by reference to the Court of Appeal's decision in Vento v Chief Constable of West Yorkshire Police [2002] EWCA Civ 1871; [2003] ICR 318 and the Employment Appeal Tribunal's decision in Da'Bell v NSPCC [2010] IRLR 19. In Vento a probationary police officer was the victim of harassment and discrimination by other police officers. She was subsequently dismissed. The applicant brought proceedings in the Employment Tribunal and recovered damages under a number of heads.

60. The Court of Appeal held that the proper award in respect of injury to feelings was £18,000. Mummery LJ delivered the judgment of the court. At paragraph 65, he gave the following guidance in relation to the assessment of damages for injury to feelings:

> "65. Employment Tribunals and those who practise in them might find it helpful if this Court were to identify three broad bands of compensation for injury to feelings, as distinct from compensation for psychiatric or similar personal injury. (i) The top band should normally be between £15,000 and £25,000. Sums in this range should be awarded in the most serious cases, such as where there has been a lengthy campaign of discriminatory harassment on the ground of sex or race. This case falls within that band. Only in the most exceptional case should an award of compensation for injury to feelings exceed £25,000. (ii) The middle band of between £5,000 and £15,000 should be used for serious cases, which do not merit an award in the highest band. (iii) Awards of between £500 and £5,000 are appropriate for less serious cases, such as where the act of discrimination is an isolated or one off occurrence. In general, awards of less than £500 are to be avoided altogether, as they risk being regarded as so low as not to be a proper recognition of injury to feelings."

61. In Da'Bell, the Employment Appeal Tribunal said that the figures in Vento should be increased for inflation as follows. The top bracket becomes £18,000 to £30,000. The second bracket becomes £6,000 to £18,000. The third bracket becomes £600 to £6,000.

62. Da'Bell was decided three years ago, therefore some further upgrading of the figures would be required to reflect inflation since 2010. For present purposes it is not necessary to do a precise calculation. It can be seen that the judge in the present case has selected a figure which is towards the bottom of the middle bracket.

63. Mr Counsell submits that the present case falls into the lowest of the three brackets; therefore the judge made an error of principle in awarding damages within the middle bracket.

64. I do not accept this submission. First, the judge, unlike this court, had the advantage of seeing and hearing the claimant give her evidence. He noted her distress when some of the phone calls were replayed in court, and he held that distress to be genuine. Secondly, when I look at the description of the three bands of cases as set out in paragraph 65 of Vento, the present case seems to me to be a classic example of a case falling within the middle band. It falls below the top band. The bank did not perpetrate a lengthy campaign of discriminatory harassment. Equally, the case falls above the bottom band. This is not a less serious case involving isolated incidents.

65. Mr Counsell submits that the bank was not deliberately targeting the claimant because of her vulnerability. This may not have been the bank's motive, but the bank was certainly targeting the claimant. Furthermore, the claimant's distress and vulnerability were made apparent to the various callers when they rang.

66. Mr Counsell submits that the bank was not making unwarranted threats. I do not agree. The threats to keep on ringing were unwarranted. It is even more unfortunate that the bank made many of these calls during a period when the claimant's credit card account would not have been overdrawn at all but for the bank's errors.

67. Mr Counsell submits that the claimant could have put an end to the calls if she had answered the bank's security questions. There are two answers to this. First, the claimant was under no obligation to answer security questions if she did not wish to talk to the bank. Secondly, I have found two instances in the transcripts where the claimant did answer the bank's security questions. That did not abate the flow of unwanted calls.

68. If I stand back from the detail and look at this case in the round, I am in entire agreement with the judge that this case falls within the middle band as defined in Vento. Where precisely the case falls within that band is a matter for the discretion of the trial judge. He alighted upon a figure of £7,500. I see no possible grounds for interfering with that assessment.

69. Accordingly, I would dismiss the appeal against quantum. I must now draw this judgment to a conclusion.

Part 7. Conclusion

70. For the reasons set out in part 5 above, I would dismiss the bank's appeal on liability. For the reasons set out in part 6 above, I would dismiss the bank's appeal on quantum of damages. If my Lady and my Lord agree, this appeal will be dismissed on all grounds.

LORD JUSTICE McCOMBE:
71. I agree, and only wish to add a few words to express my own clear view that the conduct of this bank in this case was such as to pass the threshold of harassment as prohibited by the Act, and well over the wrong side of the "sensible lines between the ordinary banter and badinage of life and genuinely offensive and unacceptable behaviour" mentioned by Lady Hale in Majrowski's case to which my Lord has already referred.

72. I only add the few words in particular because of the express plea appearing in paragraph 5 of the bank's defence and counter_claim to the following effect:

> "At all times, the telephone calls made and the letters sent by the Bank, together with the face to face contact between the claimant and the Bank's employees or agents constituted a reasonable and necessary means by which the Bank kept in contact with a customer, the Claimant, who was in arrears in respect of her accounts and were measures which were consistent with good banking practice."

73. For my part, like the judge, I was shocked by the content of some of these calls. Further, the sheer number of the calls, coupled with the express threat of repetition until the bank's wishes were complied with, was, in my judgment, wholly unacceptable. The conduct was, as the judge said, intimidatory and controlling. In short, it was, in my judgment, obviously unlawful harassment. If that amounts to good banking practice, that is a very sorry misassessment by the banks of what commercial morality and indeed legality requires. If banks wish to employ automated systems of the type used here, they need to exercise considerably more care before the automation is triggered to the extent employed in this case.

74. I agree with my Lord also that the level of damages awarded was fully appropriate on the authorities, for the clear distress which the judge found had been, and I use the word consciously, inflicted by the bank on someone who was supposed to be its customer.

75. For those additional reasons, I agree that this appeal should be dismissed.

LADY JUSTICE ARDEN:

76. I also agree. I would add this. The bank should respect the rule of law and therefore it should, in the light of the judgments of this court, revise its systems and desist from any tortious conduct, and not simply factor into its working and operating costs the fact that from time to time the bank will have to pay damages for harassment.

77. I also add this: I particularly wish to stress the importance of the context in which alleged acts of harassment occur. As my Lord, Jackson LJ, has explained, section 1(1) of the Protection from Harassment Act 1997 provides that a person must not pursue a course of conduct (a) which amounts to harassment of another, and (b) which he knows or ought to have known amounts to harassment of the other. Then in sub_section (2) it provides this, which is important for my point:

> " (2) For the purposes of this section, the person whose course of conduct is in question ought to know that it amounts to harassment of another if a reasonable person in possession of the same information would think the course of conduct amounted to harassment of the other. "

78. In Sunderland County Council v Conn [2007] EWCA Civ 46 at paragraph 12, which is quoted by Jacob LJ in Ferguson v British Gas Trading at section 5 of the bundle of authorities, Gage LJ held as follows:

> "It seems to me that what, in the words of Lord Nicholls in Majrowski, crosses the boundary between unattractive and even unreasonable conduct and conduct which is oppressive and unacceptable, may well depend on the context in which the conduct occurs. What might not be harassment on the factory floor or in the barrack room might well be harassment in the hospital ward and vice versa. In my judgment the touchstone for recognizing what is not harassment for the purposes of sections 1 and 3 will be whether the conduct is of such gravity as to justify the sanctions of the criminal law."

79. Those observations about the context, although expressed perhaps tentatively, in my judgment express the law on this point, and in that I agree with the observations made by my Lord, Jackson LJ. In my judgment, section 1(2) clearly requires the court to take into account the full context of which the defendant is aware. The context included, in the present case of course, the identity of the person receiving the call, in this case a single lady with some financial problems, receiving calls on her private phone at home, some times in the evening. I need not amplify that point because in all the circumstances of the case, the bank could not assume that a person in the respondent's position would be unaffected simply because it might be water off a duck's back for a person in some other walk of life such as a commercial person.

80. Judges hearing these cases will have to take account of all the circumstances in order to assess whether section 1(2) is satisfied. There were of course in this case many other factors such as the state of account between the parties, the state of the correspondence and the respondent's declared wish not to enter into discussions with the bank. All those considerations have been considered in my Lord Jackson LJ's judgment with which I agree.

81. It follows that because the judge had to make an evaluation of a number of detailed factors, and from the fact that this court has to respect the primary advantage that the judge had of actually hearing the testimony and in this case the tapes which recorded some of the conversations, it will be difficult for an appellant to succeed in an appellate court without showing that the judge was plainly wrong, and it is not enough therefore to try to persuade the court that it should come to some other conclusion, or that it would prefer itself to have come to some other conclusion. That is not in fact this case. I agree with my Lord that it is a plain case.

82. Those are my further observations. I agree with the order that my Lord, Jackson LJ, proposed.

Order: Appeal dismissed

Neutral Citation Number: [2009] EWCA Civ 46

Case No: A2/2008/1731

IN THE SUPREME COURT OF JUDICATURE
COURT OF APPEAL (CIVIL DIVISION)
ON APPEAL FROM THE HIGH COURT OF JUSTICE
QUEEN'S BENCH DIVISION
HIS HONOUR JUDGE SEYMOUR QC
(SITTING AS A JUDGE OF THE HIGH COURT)
HQ08X01805

Royal Courts of Justice
Strand, London, WC2A 2LL

Date: 10/02/2009

Before :

THE RT HON LORD JUSTICE SEDLEY
THE RT HON LORD JUSTICE JACOB
and
THE RT HON LORD JUSTICE LLOYD
- - - - - - - - - - - - - - - - - - - -
Between :

Lisa Maria Angela Ferguson	Claimant/ Respondent
- and -	
British Gas Trading Ltd	Defendant/ Appellant

- - - - - - - - - - - - - - - - - - - -
(Transcript of the Handed Down Judgment of
WordWave International Limited
A Merrill Communications Company
190 Fleet Street, London EC4A 2AG
Tel No: 020 7404 1400, Fax No: 020 7831 8838
Official Shorthand Writers to the Court)
- - - - - - - - - - - - - - - - - - - -
Martin Porter QC (instructed by Messrs Davis & Co) for the Appellant
James Purnell (instructed by Messrs Shepherd & Wedderburn) for the Respondent

Hearing date: 21 January 2009
- - - - - - - - - - - - - - - - - - - -
Judgment

Lord Justice Jacob:

1.   It is one of the glories of this country that every now and then one of its citizens is prepared to take a stand against the big battalions of government or industry. Such a person is Lisa Ferguson, the claimant in this case. Because she funds the claim out of her personal resources, she does so at considerable risk: were she ultimately to lose she would probably have to pay British Gas's considerable costs. I call the defendant "British Gas", its full name being "British Gas Trading Limited."

2.   Ms Ferguson used to be a customer of British Gas. She says she ceased to be so on 25th May 2006, on the same day becoming a customer of nPower. In her Particulars of Claim she sets out what she says British Gas did to her thereafter. Because the detail is lengthy I set out the relevant part of the Particulars in full in the Annex to this judgment rather than burden the reader with it here.

3.   To summarise, starting on 21st August 2006 and continuing until at least late January the next year, British Gas sent Ms Ferguson bill after bill and threatening letter after threatening letter. Nothing she could do would stop it. The threats were threefold in nature: those to cut off her gas supply, to start legal proceedings and, a matter most important to her as a businesswoman, to report her to her credit rating agencies. She wrote letter after letter pointing out that she had no account with British Gas, she made phone calls (with all the difficulty of getting through), but to no avail. Mainly her letters received no response. Sometimes she received apologies and assurances that the matter would be dealt with. But then the bills and threats continued. She complained to Energy Watch. She wrote to the Chairman of British Gas twice with no response. She says she wasted many hours, and, more importantly, was brought to a state of considerable anxiety, not knowing whether the gas man would come at any time to cut her off, whether she would have legal proceedings served upon her or whether she would be or had already been reported to a credit rating agency. Even when her solicitor wrote on her behalf about an unjustified bill of 18th January, no response was received.

4.   Ms Ferguson claims that British Gas's course of conduct amounts to unlawful harassment contrary to the Protection from Harassment Act 1997. She claims £5,000 for distress and anxiety and £5,000 for financial loss due to time lost and expenses in dealing with British Gas. She is open about her reason for bringing these proceedings. It is mainly not to claim damages for herself - she says she will give a substantial proportion of any sum awarded to charity. Ms Ferguson's principal object is to bring British Gas to book. In her words they should "not simply blame information technology. They should instead start taking responsibility for the running of their company in a competent, honest and ethical manner."

5.   British Gas says it has done nothing wrong; that it is perfectly all right for it to treat consumers in this way, at least if it is all just done by computer. It goes so far as to say that the claim is so weak that Ms Ferguson's Particulars of Claim disclose no reasonable ground for bringing it. So the claim should be struck out and not even allowed to go to trial.

6.   I note in passing that, having set out on a strike-out course, quite wrongly British Gas put in evidence consisting of two witness statements to support its application, the sort of material that might be adduced in evidence at trial. This of coursed added unnecessarily to the legal costs. Mr. Martin Porter QC for British Gas properly did not seek to rely upon this evidence. Nor, seemingly, was any attempt made to rely upon it below. But of course Ms Ferguson's legal team could not realistically completely ignore this material. That will have cost her money and increased the pressure upon her. It is an unattractive aspect of this case which fortunately no longer matters since by our decision (communicated at the end of the hearing) and the decision below, British Gas has been ordered to pay her costs both of the hearing below and here. These are not insubstantial, though they are less than those of British Gas, whose claim for costs in this Court alone (if they had won) amounted to £20,368.75. Below, British Gas was ordered to pay £10,575.

7.   As I have said, British Gas applied to strike out the claim. The case was transferred from Bromley County Court to the High Court for this application to be considered, presumably because the parties considered that a question of some importance was at stake. The strike-out application was heard and decided by HHJ Seymour QC sitting as a Deputy High Court Judge. He refused to strike out the claim, refused permission to appeal and transferred the case back to the County Court.

8.   British Gas sought and obtained from Hughes LJ permission to appeal to this Court.   Hughes LJ granted permission saying "however lamentable and frustrating the conduct of the Defendants, it is arguable that taken at its highest, it does not pass the criminal threshold."

9.   Before us Mr Porter takes that point (which he called the "gravity test").   He takes a further, more technical point, about whether, given the fact that the defendant is a company, it can be liable on the matter pleaded (the "corporate liability point").

The Legislation

10.   The relevant language of the Protection from Harassment Act reads as follows:

Prohibition of harassment.

1(1) A person must not pursue a course of conduct—

(a) which amounts to harassment of another, and

(b) which he knows or ought to know amounts to harassment of the other.

(2) For the purposes of this section, the person whose course of conduct is in question ought to know that it amounts to harassment of another if a reasonable person in possession of the same information would think the course of conduct amounted to harassment of the other.

Offence of harassment.

2(1) A person who pursues a course of conduct in breach of section 1 is guilty of an offence.

(2) A person guilty of an offence under this section is liable on summary conviction to imprisonment for a term not exceeding six months, or a fine not exceeding level 5 on the standard scale, or both.

Civil remedy.

3(1) An actual or apprehended breach of section 1 may be the subject of a claim in civil proceedings by the person who is or may be the victim of the course of conduct in question.

(2) On such a claim, damages may be awarded for (among other things) any anxiety caused by the harassment and any financial loss resulting from the harassment.

Interpretation of this group of sections

7(1)   This section applies for the interpretation of sections 1 to 5A

(2)   References to harassing a person included alarming the person or causing the person distress

The Gravity test

11.   Mr Porter accepted that what British Gas did to Ms Ferguson amounted to "a course of conduct." But, he submitted, it was not enough even arguably to amount to "harassment". No reasonable court could so conclude and hence the claim was without reasonable foundation.

12.   He pointed out that harassment is both a civil wrong (s.3(1)) and a crime (s.2(1)). That showed, he said, that the impugned conduct had to be rather serious. For otherwise merely annoying or

aggravating matters of everyday life would be criminalised, which cannot have been the intention of Parliament.

13.   In support of his contention he took us to *Majrowski v Guys and St. Thomas's NHS Trust* [2007] AC 224 and *Sunderland v Conn* [2008] EWCA Civ.148.

14.   The actual point at issue in *Majrowski* was whether an employer could be vicariously liable for harassment by acts of its employee. The House of Lords held that it could. However in the course of his reasoning Lord Nicholls observed at [30]:

> Courts are well able to separate the wheat from the chaff at an early stage of the proceedings. They should be astute to do so. In most cases courts should have little difficulty in applying the "close connection" test. Where the claim meets that requirement, and the quality of the conduct said to constitute harassment is being examined, courts will have in mind that irritations, annoyances, even a measure of upset, arise at times in everybody's day-to-day dealings with other people. Courts are well able to recognise the boundary between conduct which is unattractive, even unreasonable, and conduct which is oppressive and unacceptable. To cross the boundary from the regrettable to the unacceptable the gravity of the misconduct must be of an order which would sustain criminal liability under section 2.

And Baroness Hale said at [66]:

> All sorts of conduct may amount to harassment. It includes alarming a person or causing her distress: section 7(2). But conduct might be harassment even if no alarm or distress were in fact caused. A great deal is left to the wisdom of the courts to draw sensible lines between the ordinary banter and badinage of life and genuinely offensive and unacceptable behaviour.

15.   The passages were taken up by this Court in *Sunderland,* which, like *Majrowski,* was concerned with alleged harassment of one employee of the defendant by another such employee – a workplace context quite absent from this case. In *Sunderland* two workplace rows between an employee and his superior were proved. Although they amounted to a "course of conduct" this Court held there was no "harassment" because they were not sufficiently grave. Gage LJ said:

> [11]   As Baroness Hale put it in her speech, harassment is left deliberately wide. Section 7, to which I have referred, points to elements which are included in harassment, namely alarming or causing distress. Speech is also included as conduct which is capable of constituting harassment. The definition of "course of conduct" means that there must be at least two such incidents of harassment to satisfy the requirements of a course of conduct. It is also in my judgment important to note that a civil claim is only available as a remedy for conduct which amounts to a breach of section 1, and so by section 2 constitutes a criminal offence. The mental element in the offence is conduct which the alleged offender knows, or ought to know, judging by the standards of what the reasonable person would think, amounts to harassment of another.

> [12]   It seems to me that what, in the words of Lord Nicholls in *Majrowski,* crosses the boundary between unattractive and even unreasonable conduct and conduct which is oppressive and unacceptable, may well depend on the context in which the conduct occurs. What might not be harassment on the factory floor or in the barrack room might well be harassment in the hospital ward and vice versa. In my judgment the touchstone for recognizing what is not harassment for the purposes of sections 1 and 3 will be whether the conduct is of such gravity as to justify the sanctions of the criminal law.

Buxton LJ said at [16]:

> More fundamentally, however, as my Lord has pointed out, there is no indication at this part of the judgment, and no (I have to say) reason to infer from the terms of the recorder's decision, that he had in mind the guidance given by Lord Nicholls in <u>Majrowski</u> as to the type of conduct that crosses the line into harassment. Crucial to that is Lord Nicholls' determination my Lord has referred to that the conduct concerned must be of an order that would sustain criminal liability, and not merely civil liability on some other register. Had the recorder had that requirement in mind when he came to this part of his judgment, it seems to me I have to say completely impossible that he would have concluded that the third incident, as it has been called, the first one relied on, could amount to harassment. But what occurred is a very long way away from anything that, in a sensible criminal regime, would lead to a prosecution, much less to a conviction

Ward LJ was to similar effect.

16.   On the other hand in *Allen v Southwark* [2008] EWCA Civ. 1478 this Court refused to strike out a claim for harassment by a tenant who (in the circumstances set out in the judgment) had been the victim of a number of wrongly issued possession proceedings.   In giving the leading judgment Longmore LJ fastened upon the phrase "oppressive and unacceptable" used by Lord Nicholls in *Majrowski*.

17.   I accept that a course of conduct must be grave before the offence or tort of harassment is proved. And that, as Mr Porter accepted after some discussion, the only real difference between the crime of s.2 and the tort of s.3 is standard of proof.   To prove the civil wrong of harassment it is necessary to prove the case on a balance of probabilities, to prove the crime, the standard is the usual criminal one of beyond a reasonable doubt.

18.   In so accepting I would just add this word of caution: the fact of parallel criminal and civil liability is not generally, outside the particular context of harassment, of significance in considering civil liability. There are a number of other civil wrongs which are also crimes.   Perhaps most common would be breaches of the Trade Descriptions Act 1968 as amended.   In the field of intellectual property both trade mark and copyright infringement, and the common law tort of passing off (which generally involves deception), may all amount to crimes.   It has never been suggested generally that the scope of a civil wrong is restricted because it is also a crime.   What makes the wrong of harassment different and special is because, as Lord Nicholls and Lady Hale recognised, in life one has to put up with a certain amount of annoyance: things have got to be fairly severe before the law, civil or criminal, will intervene.

19.   Having accepted Mr Porter's submission about the legal test requiring gravity, I apply it here. I am quite unable to conclude that the impugned conduct is incapable of satisfying the test. On the contrary I think, at the very least, that it is strongly arguable that it does. I ask myself whether a jury or bench of magistrates could reasonably conclude that the persistent and continued conduct here pleaded was on the wrong side of the line, as amounting to "oppressive and unacceptable conduct".   I am bound to say that I think they could. And, in contrast to the *Sunderland* case, for instance, I would think it entirely proper for a prosecutor such as a Trading Standards Officer, to bring criminal proceedings in respect of a case where there has been such a period of persistent conduct and such threats as are pleaded here.

20.   What British Gas was threatening was undoubtedly serious.   Mr Porter sought to downgrade it by saying that Ms Ferguson knew the claims and threats were unjustified.   That is absurd: a victim of harassment will almost always know that it is unjustified. The Act is there to protect people against unjustified harassment.   Indeed if the impugned conduct is justified it is unlikely to amount to harassment at all.

21.   Mr Porter also made the point that the correspondence was computer generated and so, for some reason which I do not really follow, Ms Ferguson should not have taken it as seriously as if it had come from an individual. But real people are responsible for programming and entering material into the computer. It is British Gas's system which, at the very least, allowed the impugned conduct to happen.

22.   Moreover the threats and demands were to be read by a real person, not by a computer.   A real person is likely to suffer real anxiety and distress if threatened in the way which Ms Ferguson was.   And a real person is unlikely to take comfort from knowing that the claims and threats are unjustified or that they were sent by a computer system: that will not necessarily allay the fear that the threats will not be carried out.   How is a consumer such as Ms Ferguson to know whether or not, for instance, a threat such as "we will tell a credit reference agency in the next 10 days that you have not paid" (letter of 2nd January) will not be carried out by the same computer system which sent the unjustified letter and all its predecessor bills and threats?   After all no amount of writing and telephoning had stopped the system so far – at times it must have seemed like a monster machine out of control moving relentlessly forward – a million miles from the "world class level of service" (letter of 9th January) which British Gas says it aims to offer.

23.   So I would reject Mr Porter's gravity point.   It must go to trial.

The corporate liability point

24.   Mr Porter submits that even if the alleged conduct as a whole, if carried out by one sentient being such as an individual trader, would amount to "harassment" it is not enough to prove a case against a large corporation.   For that, he submitted, the claimant must prove more.   She must plead either that the course of conduct was directed by someone with seniority in the company (e.g. a director) that that person's mind is regarded as the mind of the company itself (a so-called "directing mind"), or that the course of conduct was the responsibility of an individual employee for whose acts the company is vicariously liable.   Neither of these, he submitted, was pleaded here, so the claim was bound to fail.

25.   He founded his submission on a single authority, *Tesco v Nattrass* [1972] AC 153.   Tesco had set up a proper system to prevent offences under the Trade Descriptions Act 1968.   But a store manager failed to check his staff who had put up a "special offer" poster for goods which were being sold at a normal price, contrary to the provisions of the Act.   The prosecution of Tesco failed.   Mr Porter took us to what was said by Lord Morris at p.179:

> How, then, does a company act? When is some act the act of the company as opposed to the act of a servant or agent of the company (for which, if done within the scope of employment, the company will be civilly answerable)?   In *Lennard's Carrying Co. Ltd. v. Asiatic Petroleum Co. Ltd.* [1915] A.C. 705 Viscount Haldane L.C. said, at p. 713:
>
>> "My Lords, a corporation is an abstraction. It has no mind of its own any more than it has a body of its own; its active and directing will must consequently be sought in the person of somebody who for some purposes may be called an agent, but who is really the directing mind and will of the corporation, the very ego and centre of the personality of the corporation. That person may be under the direction of the shareholders in general meeting; that person may be the board of directors itself, or it may be, and in some companies it is so, that that person has an authority co-ordinate with the board of directors given to him under the articles of association, and is appointed by the general meeting of the company, and can only be removed by the general meeting of the company."

26.   This showed, he said, that there is a general rule: in all cases there has to be directing mind or an identifiable employee for whom the company is vicariously liable.   That rule is, he submitted, applicable here.

27.   But *Tesco v Nattrass*, as also *Lennard's* to which Lord Morris referred, turned on the provisions of the particular Act with which each case was concerned.   In *Lennard's* the question was whether a ship-owner company was liable for loss of a cargo destroyed by a fire caused by the defective boilers of the owner's ship which was accordingly unseaworthy.   There would be liability unless s.502 of the Merchant Shipping Act 1894 applied.   For that it was necessary to show that the loss happened "without his actual fault or privity."   The individual entrusted with the management of the ship knew or had the means of knowledge of the defects, but took no steps about them and allowed the ship to go

to sea.   The House of Lords held the defence failed because the individual concerned should be regarded as the directing mind of the company.

28.   It is noteworthy that the House took the view that it was for the company to prove the defence and that its failure to call the individual to explain what had happened was fatal.   In this case one is unable to say whether British Gas would be in a position to escape liability on a "directing mind" basis since we have no evidence about it.   One simply does not know whether what happened to Ms Ferguson is an extraordinary one-off case, or whether there are so many similar cases that senior management must know about it but are prepared to tolerate the position because it brings in the money.   And even if liability can be avoided on that basis, there is the real potential for liability on the "ought to know" basis – see below.

29.   *Tesco v Nattrass* turned on the particular provisions of the 1968 Act.   The question before the House was whether Tesco could rely upon s.24(1).   This provided a defence for a person charged to prove (a) that the commission of the offence was due to … the act or default of another person .. and (b) that he took all reasonable precautions and exercised all due diligence to avoid the commission of such an offence.   S.24(1)(b) was satisfied because Tesco had set up reasonable precautions, so the question was whether the store manager was "another person" within the meaning of s.24(1)(b).   It was held he was.

30.   Even when *Tesco v Nattrass* was cited in argument before us, it seemed a long way from this case.   The provisions of the Trade Descriptions Act and the Protection from Harassment Act are quite, quite different.   But there is more.   We were conscious at the time that perhaps we had not had as full a citation of authority about corporate liability as might be appropriate.   So we asked one of our judicial assistants to look into the matter.   She found a host of further, post-*Tesco v Nattrass* material indicating quite strongly that it was a case confined to the language of the particular statute being considered.

31.   I do not think it right, on an incompletely argued strike-out application, to analyse all this material in detail.   Nor to come to anything other than a provisional conclusion about the question of corporate liability under the Act.   What I will do is to identify all the material identified for us, consider what at present seem to be the two most material cases, and then say what my provisional view as to the meaning of this Act is.

32.   The material identified is *Essendon Engineering v Maile* [1982] Crim. L.R. 510; *Group Newspapers v SOGAT* [1987] I.C.R. 181; *Tesco v Brent* [1993] 1 W.L.R. 1037; *Re Supply of Ready Mixed Concrete (No.2)* [1995] 1 A.C. 456; *Meridian Global Funds Management Asia v Securities Commission* [1995] 2 A.C. 500; *Re British Steel* [1995] 1 W.L.R. 1356; and *Cambridgeshire CC v Kama* [2006] EWHC 3148.

33.   In *Meridian,* Lord Hoffmann said this at p.507:

> The fact that the rule of attribution is a matter of interpretation or construction of the relevant substantive rule is shown by the contrast between two decisions of the House of Lords, *Tesco Supermarkets Ltd. v. Nattrass* and *In re Supply of Ready Mixed Concrete (No. 2).*

He went on to describe each of these cases and a number of others.   At p.511 he said:

> The question is one of construction rather than metaphysics

And:

> But their Lordships would wish to guard themselves against being understood to mean that whenever a servant of a company has authority to do an act on its behalf, knowledge of that act will for all purposes be attributed to the company. It is a question of construction in each case as to whether the particular rule requires that the knowledge that an act has been done, or the state of mind with which it was done, should be attributed to the company. Sometimes, as in *In re Supply of Ready Mixed Concrete (No. 2)* [1995] 1 A.C. 456 and this case, it will be appropriate. Likewise in a case

in which a company was required to make a return for revenue purposes and the statute made it an offence to make a false return with intent to deceive, the Divisional Court held that the mens rea of the servant authorised to discharge the duty to make the return should be attributed to the company: see *Moore v. I. Bresler Ltd.* [1944] 2 All E.R. 515. On the other hand, the fact that a company's employee is authorised to drive a lorry does not in itself lead to the conclusion that if he kills someone by reckless driving, the company will be guilty of manslaughter. There is no inconsistency. Each is an example of an attribution rule for a particular purpose, tailored as it always must be to the terms and policies of the substantive rule.

34.   That makes it entirely clear that one cannot just jump from one Act to another and say the rule for one is the rule for the other.

35.   And even with legislation affecting the conduct of retail trade, the position differs depending on the particular provision in question. This appears from the second Tesco case, *Tesco v Brent.* Tesco sold a video marked "18" to a 14-year old, contrary to s.11 of the Video Recordings Act 1984. S.11(2) provided a defence that the accused "neither knew or had reasonable grounds to believe" that the person was under age. The Divisional Court rejected a defence based on the fact that Tesco as a company did not know anything about the age of the purchaser. It reasoned that Parliament would know that the management of a company could not know anything about the age of a particular purchaser, and so the relevant factor was the knowledge of the employee involved in the transaction. *Tesco v Nattrass* was distinguished for a variety of reasons. I do not spell them all out here save to note that one of them was the fact that the court was concerned with different Acts, different language and different policies.

36.   It is however worth picking up two short passages from the judgment of Staughton LJ. At p. 1042 he said:

> The language here draws no distinction between the defendant and those under his control. The content is concerned with knowledge and information, not due diligence.

That is also true of the Protection from Harassment Act.

37.   The other passage is a single sentence at p. 1043:

> I cannot believe that Parliament intended the large company to be acquitted but the single-handed shopkeeper convicted.

That also seems applicable to the Protection from Harassment Act. For here British Gas, upon the assumption that the course of conduct amounts to harassment, accept that a single trader guilty of the same conduct would be liable.

38.   Finally, therefore, I turn to what I conceive to be the critical question, namely the construction of this Act. These are my provisional views only. As I have said the corporate liability point was not fully argued. And besides this point would be better decided after all the facts are known.

39.   The key words are in s.1(1)(b):

> he knows or ought to know amounts to harassment of the other;

And in s1(2):

> For the purposes of this section, the person whose course of conduct is in question ought to know that it amounts to harassment of another if a reasonable person in possession of the same information would think the course of conduct amounted to harassment of the other.

40.   It is to be noted that the Act does not provide any defence for "accidental" harassment. Nor does it contain anything like s.24 of the Trade Descriptions Act, considered in *Tesco v Nattrass*. And one cannot think of any policy reason why big corporations should be exonerated for conduct which, if carried out by an individual, would amount to harassment.

41.   So Ms Ferguson must show either that British Gas *knew* the conduct complained of amounted to harassment, or that it *ought* to have so known.

42.   So far as a case based on actual knowledge is concerned, that would require proof of knowledge of the conduct and that it amounted to harassment. I am inclined towards the view that Ms Ferguson has pleaded enough to allege knowledge of the conduct complained of. For as a matter of construction it seems a company must be taken to have knowledge of material within the knowledge of its employees, even if top management know nothing of the particular case. That is particularly so where, as here, the company may be liable vicariously, see *Majrowski*. But there may be difficulties on showing knowledge that the conduct amounted to harassment. That would in itself potentially depend on how frequently this sort of thing has been happening and how aware senior management was aware of it. If, as I hope is not the case, it was known to be happening regularly and it had been decided that it was nonetheless worth it, then I can envisage Ms Ferguson getting home on actual knowledge.

43.   At this stage of course we have no idea of what the state of British Gas's actual knowledge was. Mr Porter suggested that was not good enough, that it is incumbent on Ms Ferguson in her particulars of claim to identify an individual with actual knowledge. That seems to me to be mistaken. Who knew what within British Gas is peculiarly within its knowledge. All Ms Ferguson can do is to identify the communications passing between British Gas and herself. If they raise, as I think they do, an arguable case of conduct amounting to harassment, then I think the onus shifts to British Gas to explain its state of knowledge.

44.   But the case on actual knowledge probably does not matter. For she does not have to go as far as to prove actual knowledge. An "ought to know" case will suffice. s.1(2) governs what amounts to this. It brings into play that well-known character "the reasonable person". As at present it seems to me that all the Act requires of the victim is to identify the course of conduct and what passed between the victim and the alleged harasser. The court is then notionally to put knowledge of that and of any other relevant information into the mind of this reasonable person. The court then decides whether that person would consider that the course of conduct amounts to harassment. Mr Porter suggested that there might be what I would call a defence of incompetence or the right hand not knowing what the left hand was doing. I am doubtful as to this as a matter of construction of the statute. The "reasonable person" is given the "same information" which, as I say, seems to be of the entire course of conduct plus the victim's responses. It is the point of view of the victim in the light of these facts which the reasonable person is to consider. The perpetrator's private reasons or excuses or explanations for the conduct do not come into it.

45.   I say no more about the corporate defence. If I am right in my provisional view, there simply is not one on the "ought to know" case. The only question at trial will be whether the conduct amounted to "harassment".

46.   We informed the parties at the conclusion of the hearing that the appeal would be dismissed. These are my reasons for so doing.

Lord Justice Lloyd:

47.   I agree with Jacob LJ that British Gas has failed to make out its primary case, that the conduct alleged is not capable of being regarded as of sufficient gravity to constitute harassment in breach of the 1997 Act. I also agree with him that the alternative ground is also not made out, namely that none of the acts alleged, or not enough of them, are to be attributed to British Gas, either directly or vicariously, so as to make it liable even if the course of conduct was sufficiently grave to amount to a breach of the Act.

48.   Like him, I consider that we should not decide what the test is for corporate responsibility under the 1997 Act, having had what we now know to be only incomplete citation of relevant decided cases. For my part it seems to me that this test is not likely to depend on the issue of actual or deemed knowledge, but on the policy issue, as a matter of the true interpretation of the Act, whether conduct carried out in

the course of the business of a particular body is to be attributed, for the purposes of this Act, to that body as a whole regardless of whether any one individual within the organisation was doing it all, or knew of it all being done, and if so at what level in the organisation that person was operating.

49. The comparison by reference to the hypothetical reasonable person which is required by section 1(2) involves deeming that person not only to be reasonable but also to be in possession of the same information as the person has who is responsible for the course of conduct. Thus, the hypothetical person is treated as knowing not only the acts that British Gas did which make up the course of conduct, but also that which Mrs Ferguson did in response, and the relevant factual context, so far as known to British Gas. This assumes that British Gas is the perpetrator of the course of conduct, directly or vicariously, but that is what is alleged by Ms Ferguson and, in agreement with Jacob LJ and for the reasons he gives, it seems to me that this is not a point on which the claim can be struck out. What the knowledge is that is to be attributed to the hypothetical reasonable person will depend on the view taken, on the facts and on the construction of the Act, as to who it is that was responsible for the course of conduct. The deeming process is dependent on the answer to the prior question; it has no relevance to the process of finding the answer to that question.

Lord Justice Sedley:

50. I agree that Judge Seymour QC was entirely right not to strike out this claim. Like Lord Justice Jacob, I think it deplorable that, both by evidence and by argument, British Gas sought below to bolster their contention that the claim on its face was incapable of succeeding with untried explanations or excuses for their conduct. It is therefore worth reiterating that the court on an application such as this is required to assume that the claimant will prove all that she has alleged and that this will be the totality of the evidence. It is only if some unrevealed but incontestable fact will render the case hopeless that evidence can be adduced in support of such an application. This apart (and nothing advanced by British Gas comes close to it), if the claim is capable of succeeding, it is at trial, if at all, that the explanations and excuses become relevant.

51. One excuse which has formed part of British Gas's legal argument for striking out the claim, and which has been advanced as incontestable and decisive, is that a large corporation such as British Gas cannot be legally responsible for mistakes made either by its computerised debt recovery system or by the personnel responsible for programming and operating it. The short answer is that it can be, for reasons explained by Lord Justice Jacob. It would be remarkable if it could not: it would mean that the privilege of incorporation not only shielded its shareholders and directors from personal liability for its debts but protected the company itself from legal liabilities which a natural person cannot evade. That is not what legal personality means.

52. Lord Justice Jacob has drawn attention to the fact that in order to bring this claim Ms Ferguson has had to put her own resources at risk. For my part I would draw attention to the fact – which has been prominent elsewhere in British Gas's argument – that harassment is a crime as well as a tort. Contrary to what was more than once suggested, this does not modify in any way the constituents of the wrong. All it means is that, on a prosecution, the identical elements must be proved not simply on the balance of probability but so that the court is sure. In any well-documented case, what is sufficient for the one purpose is likely to be sufficient for the other.

53. Parliament's intention in passing the Protection from Harassment Act 1997 was to criminalise the kind of serious and persistent unwarranted threat which is alleged here, giving a right of civil action as a fallback. In this situation it ought not to be left to hardy individuals to put their savings and homes at risk by suing. The primary responsibility should rest upon local public authorities which possess the means and the statutory powers to bring alleged harassers, however impersonal and powerful, before the local justices.

Annex: the full Particulars of Claim

1. The Claimant, a self-employed property investor, had a domestic gas supply contract with the Defendant. She closed this account on 25 May 2006 and changed gas supplier to npower on that date.

2.   The Claimant received a letter from npower dated 16 August 2006, confirming that her gas supply had been transferred to npower on 25 May 2006.

3.   On receipt of the letter referred to in paragraph 2 above, the Claimant telephoned npower because she had not received a closing statement from the Defendant. Npower again confirmed that the data had been passed to the Defendant.

4.   The Claimant received a bill from the Defendant dated 21 August 2006 in the amount of £236.40 for the period 14 April 2006 to 14 July 2006.

5.   On receiving a reminder from the Defendant dated 11 September 2006 relating to the above bill, the Claimant made several unsuccessful attempts to speak to the Defendant by telephone. The Claimant then posted a copy of the reminder to the Defendant annotated in bold, stating that the bill was invalid as the account was closed. No response was received to that letter.

6.   On 29 September 2006 the Claimant telephoned npower, who confirmed that the transfer data had been passed to the Defendant on two occasions.

7.   The Claimant received a letter from the Defendant dated 25 September 2006, threatening gas disconnection. The Claimant wrote to the Defendant stating that the account was closed and enclosing a copy of the letter from npower referred to in paragraph 2 above.

8.   On 4 October 2006, the Claimant wrote to the gas and electricity watchdog Energywatch to advise them of the problems she was experiencing with the Defendant.

9.   The Claimant received a bill from the Defendant dated 29 September 2006 in the amount of £158.23 for the period 14 April 2006 to 23 May 2006 in respect of 170 units up to a reading of 0517. The Claimant paid this bill in full on 10 October 2006, believing it to be her closing bill as it covered the correct period up to the transfer of her supply from the Defendant to npower.

10.   The Claimant received a letter from the Defendant dated 19 October 2006, acknowledging receipt of £158.23 and stating that her account was paid in full. The Claimant believed that the problems with the Defendant had now been resolved. She had paid the Defendant in full for all services received prior to her transfer to npower.

11.   The Claimant then received a bill from the Defendant dated 20 November 2006 for the period 24 May 2006 to 13 October 2006 in the amount of £253.31. The Defendant sent a reminder on 11 December 2006 in respect of this bill.

12.   On 20 December 2006, the Claimant returned the bill referred to in paragraph 10 above to the Admail Customer Complaints Manager with a covering letter. No response was received.

13.   On 4 January 2007, the Claimant received a letter from the Defendant dated 25 December 2006, threatening the Claimant with gas disconnection and warning that her credit rating might be blacklisted.

14.   The Claimant then received a letter dated 2 January 2007 from the Defendant's Head of Debt stating that legal action was being arranged, that the gas supply at her property would be disconnected on or after 29 January 2007, that the Claimant's credit rating might be adversely affected, that the Defendant would notify a credit reference agency in the next 10 days if the Claimant had not paid the sums due, and that further legal action might be taken which could result in considerable legal costs and/or transfer of the debt to a debt collection agency.

15.   On 5 January 2007, in alarm and distress following receipt of the threatening letter dated 2 January 2007 the Claimant, after sending a fax to Energywatch stressing the urgency of her situation, contacted her solicitor for advice.

16. On 9 January 2007 the Claimant wrote to the Defendant's Head of Debt, advising him that she had instructed her solicitor and requesting that all future correspondence be copied to her solicitor. No response was received.

17. The Defendant sent a letter dated 5 January 2007 to the Claimant, confirming the transfer of supply on 25 May 2006 at a reading of 0517 and asking the Claimant to ignore the reminder dated 11 December 2006. There was no reference to the letter of 2 January.

18. The Claimant received a letter of apology from the Defendant dated 9 January 2007 which stated that it was in response to her complaint to Energywatch. This letter confirmed that the Claimant's gas supply had left the Defendant on 25 May 2006 at a reading of 0517, that a bill which had been issued on 5 January had been cancelled and that the Claimant was to ignore this bill when it arrived. There was no reference to their letter of 2 January 2007.

19. On 10 January 2007, the Claimant replied to the Defendant's letter of 9 January 2007 enclosing a copy of her letter to the Defendant's Head of Debt referred to in paragraph 16 above. No response was received.

20. On 15 January 2007, the Claimant's solicitor wrote to the Defendant seeking an undertaking that they would cease chasing payment of wrongly issued bills, withdraw all threats of legal action against the Claimant and refrain from taking any steps to enter the Claimant's property. No response was received.

21. On 17 January 2007 the Claimant received two bills dated 9 January 2007 from the Defendant, each in the amount of £0.28. One of these bills was marked "final bill". 179 units were billed up to a reading of 0517. This was the same closing reading shown on the bill dated 29 September 2006 up to the date of transfer of the Claimant's supply, which the Claimant had already paid.

22. On 24 January 2007, the Claimant sent a fax to Energywatch enclosing recent correspondence with the Defendant including the Defendant's letter of 2 January 2007 referred to in paragraph 14 above and the bill dated 18 January 2007.

23. On 25 January 2007, the Claimant's solicitor wrote to the Defendant asking them to rectify the errors in the bills referred to in paragraph 21 above. No reply was received.

24. On 24 January 2007, the Claimant received a bill dated 18 January 2007 from the Defendant for the period 14 April to 13 October 2006 in the sum of £253.31. This bill has not been cancelled. This is the most recent written communication from the Defendant.

25. On 30 January 2007 and 3 March 2007, the Claimant sent letters to the Defendant's Chairman by recorded delivery setting out details of her harassment by the Defendant and her intention to raise a claim against the Defendant. No reply has been received to either letter.

CHRISTOPHER MERVYN PONCELET -v- NPOWER LIMITED

APPROVED JUDGMENT

JUDGE BRAY:

1. This is a claim brought for harassment by the Claimant, Mr. Poncelet. The very brief background is that he was a customer of npower and he had transferred from British Gas to npower to provide him with his electricity. Mr. Poncelet, if he will forgive me for saying so, is a somewhat unusual person, because he works at night a great deal of the time, whereas most of us work during the day. That has a significant effect in relation to the provision of electricity, because as most of us know, the major suppliers of electricity charge at different rates. They charge at a higher rate per day and a lower rate per night, it is sometimes called "The economy rate". That is well-known. Therefore, Mr. Poncelet, who works very often throughout the night or late at night, is in a somewhat different position to the rest of us.

2. Nevertheless, that is not a matter which should excuse the electricity provider. They have to deal with whatever customer they have, and to send the appropriate bills. It became very apparent in this case, unfortunately, that npower were not fulfilling their responsibility to send appropriate bills to Mr. Poncelet. Far from it. The main problem I have already alluded to, and that is that consistently they were charging him for electricity used during the night as if he had been using it during the day, doubtless because they were not used, perhaps, to such a customer. However, as I have already said, that is no excuse.

3. I am not going to go into the whole history of the matter, because it extends over a great deal of time and involves a great many complaints which Mr. Poncelet has set out in his witness statement, and which are contained also in the skeleton argument. It

1

is sufficient to say that as soon as he realised that mistakes were consistently being made, he repeatedly got in contact with npower to complain, to point out their mistakes and to ask them to put it right. Though on occasions there were claims that they were going to put it right, they never did so, and they never did so over a lengthy period of time.

4.   It did not just stop there, because frequently when Mr. Poncelet phoned to complain he was cut off in suspicious circumstances, as if npower were saying "We can't deal with customers who complain. They're a nuisance, and we're simply going to cut them off". That was the effect that it doubtless had on Mr. Poncelet, who became more and more anxious and concerned, and when it came to demands for payment and the threats that were made to him, frightened as well. There were threats from agents of debt-collecting agencies. There were threats that he was going to be taken to the Magistrates' Court, effectively. There were threats that his electricity was going to be cut off, all of which, upon a perfectly innocent customer, must have had a very serious effect and a cumulative effect over a period of three years.

5.   Now, I am not going to go further into the detail save to just mention one final matter, which was that up to a matter of a few days ago, as I understand it, there was still a dispute as to whether Mr. Poncelet owed npower money for electricity. However, apparently a letter or a document was provided as late as last week with a reconciliation which shows that far from him owing npower, they actually owed him a small amount of money, which was then cancelled out by a claim for £23, as I recall, for a debt collector having to come and knock at the door. If there was ever adding insult to injury, that was it.

6.   I turn from that to consider the legal requirements that have to be fulfilled by a Claimant in order to successfully claim damages for harassment. There are, it

2

appears, three essential requirements. Firstly, there must be a course of conduct; there plainly has been a course of conduct here over a number of years. Secondly, the course of conduct must cause harassment to another. I am quite satisfied that harassment has been caused here. I have considered the test for harassment, and of course harassment here is something that must be serious. It has got to be something, since this essentially was a criminal act which provides civil remedies, that falls at the high end of misconduct. It has already been defined in the case of *Ferguson* as oppressive and unacceptable conduct.

7.   I have considered carefully the submissions of Mr. Radley-Davies here. He was engagingly frank in what he had to say to me, and he accepted that the conduct of npower was abominable. I am quite satisfied that not only was it abominable, but it constituted harassment, as being oppressive and unacceptable conduct by a large company upon a small, if you will forgive me for saying so, individual. So I am satisfied that it meets the test of seriousness and constitutes harassment.

8.   Finally, it has got to be established that the harasser must know or ought to know that the course of conduct amounts to harassment. Here it is said that npower believed that the money was owing. It may be that they did, but they ought to have known that it was not owing because they had repeated complaints from the Claimant here. If they had bothered to make even the most cursory checks, they would have found out that his claims were correct. It is sad to have to hear that he was reduced to having CCTV outside his property and make photographic evidence of visits from the meter readers.

9.   So I am quite satisfied that the claim is established. The proof required is the balance of probabilities. Even if it were the criminal proof, I am quite sure that this matter has been made out, and the claim succeeds.

3

10. The case of *Ferguson* has been cited before me. I am not going to go into it beyond the first sentence, which I feel obliged to repeat because it is so true. That it is "... one of the glories of this country that every now and then one of its citizens is prepared to take a stand against the big battalions of government or industry ..." That is what the Court of Appeal felt in the case of *Ferguson*, and that is what I now find in this particular case as well.

11. As to damages, Mr. Tilley has not sought to have his pound of flesh here, in the sense that all he wants is a declaration that he is entitled to switch his account now to another provider, that having been refused to him because of a false claim that he owed npower money. Doubtless, if npower had transferred the account or agreed to have the account transferred, we would never be here at this Court. It is only because of the way he has been treated that he has brought the claim.

12. I am quite satisfied that he has suffered a lot as a result of this, sadly, and it is not just a question of writing him a letter and giving him an apology, it has gone beyond that now. As I understand the law, damages are available under the tort of harassment for anxiety, and I have listened carefully to the evidence given to me today from the Claimant. It is quite obvious that he has suffered a great deal of anxiety as a result of this case. He has not been able to sleep properly. He has had to spend hours, I think he gave a total of somewhere around 300 hours, answering letters. He felt that if he did not answer them, then they would regard the bills as being accepted, and I can well understand that. I can well picture the suffering that he has had to undergo over a considerable period. We are not talking about six months here, we are talking about up to three years.

13. He has been on tranquillisers. Now, I appreciate that he was taking tranquillisers before this situation arose in 2007, for other reasons. However, it is clear law that any

Defendant must take his victim as he finds him, and if Mr. Poncelet was a vulnerable person, as he plainly was, for whatever reason, then under the eggshell skull principle the tortfeasor, or harasser in this case, must take the responsibility for that. So it is a factor I bear in mind in awarding damages in this case.

14. General damages are being claimed, and of course that is not an entirely easy issue in a case of this sort to assess. No cases specifically on the point have been raised before me. *Ferguson*, of course, was only on the question of whether a claim in principle lay, not on the quantum of damages. I know not whether this is the first case in which such an assessment falls to be made, but obviously some comparison must be made with psychiatric injuries, for example. I have had recourse to the guidelines set out by the Judicial Studies Board. This obviously falls at the lower end, and taking a bracket which is set out in the assessment at 1,000 to 3,800, I know it is in different circumstances, but it seems to me not an unreasonable bracket for a case of this sort.

15. Doing the best that I can in all the circumstances, I am going to award a sum of £3,000 here.

IN THE HIGH COURT OF JUSTICE
CHANCERY DIVISION

Case No: 8MA 30188

Civil Justice Centre Manchester

Date: 13/07/2009

Before :

THE HON MR JUSTICE NICOL

- -

Between :

S & D Property Investments Ltd	Claimant
- and -	Part 20 Defendant
Christian Nisbet	Defendant
Stephen French	Part 20
	Claimant/Defendant

- -
- -

Ms Cheryl Dainty of Counsel instructed by **Pannone Solicitors** for the **Claimant and Part 20 Defendant**
Mr Kenderik Horne of Counsel instructed by **JST Lawyers Solicitors for** for the Defendant

Hearing dates: 22.06.09, 23.06.09 and 1.07.09
- -
Judgment

The Honourable Mr Justice Nicol :

1. The case of *Nisbet v French* began in the Liverpool County Court on 22nd January 2008. Mr Nisbet sought an injunction and damages against Mr French under the Protection from Harassment Act 1997. An injunction for a limited period was granted the same day, but was later extended. On 16th April 2008 proceedings began in the Manchester District Registry in the case of *S & D Property Investments Ltd v Nisbet*. This was a debt action for a principal sum of £111,579.53 plus interest which were said to be due from Mr Nisbet. Mr French owns 50% of the shares in, and is one of the two directors of, S & D Property Investments Ltd ('S&D'). The remaining shares are owned by his wife, Dionne, who is the other director. Indeed, that company's name is an allusion to the initial letters of Stephen and Dionne French. In his Defence and Counterclaim of 27th May 2008 Mr Nisbet admitted the debt but sought to counterclaim damages for harassment of Mr French for which he said S & D was vicariously liable. He argued that the counterclaim should be set off in extinction or diminution of S & D's claim.

2. On 26th March 2009 judgment was entered by consent for S & D in the sum of £135,481.39 inclusive of the interest that had by then accumulated together with further interest at the contractual rate of 20% until payment. However, enforcement of that judgment sum was stayed until the outcome of the trial of the two actions (which were also consolidated) or further order. To avoid confusion I will refer to the parties by their names.

3. Shortly before the trial date, Mr Nisbet applied for permission to adduce expert evidence. It was an important part of his case that the alleged harassment of Mr French, in addition to causing him anxiety and distress, had led to economic loss. Two of his companies, Albany Assets Ltd ('Assets') and Albany Crown Ltd. ('Crown') had been engaged in negotiations for the development of a site in Manchester. He alleged that Mr French's harassment had made him unable to devote the time and energy which this project needed, it had been delayed or otherwise prejudiced as a result and he, as the only shareholder in Assets and Crown, had suffered loss in consequence. The expert evidence which he wished to adduce would have gone to the quantification of that loss. S & D and Mr French opposed the application which, they said, would have delayed the trial and thereby unduly extended the period for which the stay on enforcement of the judgment debt would operate.

4. On 12th June HHJ Stephen Davies did not authorise the service of expert evidence. However, he directed that the trial should proceed:

'in relation to all issues other than quantification of any financial loss alleged by Mr Nisbet to have been caused due to delay to the Manchester hotel development project. For the avoidance of doubt, the trial shall deal with all issues other than quantification of financial loss, including:

    i.   whether or not S & D Properties is vicariously liable;

    ii.   whether or not any harassment caused any delay;

    iii.   whether or not S & D Properties or Mr French are liable in law for any financial loss due to delay to the Manchester hotel project.'

5.   It is this trial which I heard in Manchester on 22nd and 23rd June and 1st July 2009.

6.   Mr French acknowledges that until the mid-1990s he had a reputation for extreme violence. He was deeply involved with gang crime in Liverpool. However, it is his case that he put all of this behind him in about 1994 and he now publicly urges those from the same sort of background as he had to give up (or not take up) guns, knives and drugs.

7.   He met Mr Nisbet in about 1996. They became friends and, to an extent, were involved in business together. One venture was Chrymark Security Ltd ('Chrymark'). Mr Nisbet eventually took this over although Mr French still had (or believed he had) an investment interest. It was not a success and became insolvent in about 2005.

8.   By then two others, Steve Moule and John Mason, had joined Mr Nisbet as directors of Chrymark. Mr French took exception to this and in April 2005 he expressed his displeasure to Mr Nisbet. Mr Nisbet's recollection was that Mr French said that he would not kill him but he would kill Messrs Moule and Mason. Mr French's recollection is that something less precise was said. It was an off-hand remark for which he apologised very shortly afterwards in a telephone call to Mr Nisbet.

9.   Three months later, on 3rd June 2005, Mr French met with Mr Nisbet and his solicitor, Heather Summers of JST Lawyers. Her handwritten contemporaneous note of the meeting says 'SF withdraws statements JM/SM'. The typed version of these notes said 'Steve French confirming that he was happy to withdraw all statements he had made to John Mason and Steve Moule especially the death threats'. Mr Nisbet relies on this as confirmation that death threats had been made. Ms Dainty, on behalf of Mr French and S&D, observes that the handwritten notes did not refer to 'death threats'. I do not regard this discrepancy as significant. The typed notes were themselves produced very shortly after the meeting. The typed version is fuller in many respects than the handwritten notes but it was prepared very shortly after the meeting when the events would still have been fresh in Ms Summers' mind. The typed notes were sent to Mr French under cover of a letter dated 9th June 2005 for his comment. He took no issue with their accuracy. Ms Summers verified the notes in a witness statement for these proceedings and no request was made for her to attend for cross examination.

10.   Mr French also appears to have invested in two other projects of Mr Nisbet's: Albany Building Ltd ('Building') and Albany Irwell Ltd ('Irwell').

11.   From about mid 2005 there appears to have been a lull in the relationship between Mr French and Mr Nisbet. In January 2007, however, their friendship and business relationship revived. Mr Nisbet says that Mr French contacted him when he was on holiday. He seemed to be a changed person.

12.   Mr Nisbet and his companies were suffering cash flow difficulties and Mr French offered to provide assistance. The loan which was the subject of the claim in the High Court proceedings was made in four tranches between March and September 2007. Mr French offered this as an interest free loan, but Mr Nisbet insisted on paying interest and at 20%.

13.   In the summer of 2007 the Building and Irwell companies also went into administration. This exacerbated Mr Nisbet's financial difficulties and, in particular, deprived him of assets out of which he had hoped to repay S&D's loans.

14.   At the end of August 2007 a book called 'The Devil' was published. Although written by someone else, it apparently relied very heavily on material supplied by Mr French. While he denied in evidence that the book was entirely autobiographical, it did describe the violent milieu of the Liverpool underworld of which Mr French had once been part.

15.   From about the end of August 2007 Mr Nisbet began to keep a record of emails, texts and telephone messages which were left or sent by Mr French. Mr French accepted in evidence that they were an accurate record.

16.   In September, Mr Nisbet's financial difficulties continued. He emailed Mr French on 2nd September 2007 asking if he could provide a further loan. Mr French seems to have responded positively because the final loan from S&D to Mr Nisbet was made on 4th September 2007. This was for £13,000. The payment was channelled through Assets. This brought the total loans made by S&D to Mr Nisbet to £118,850.

17.   Mr French had two other investment possibilities at about this time. One was a property in Turkey which Mr French saw as an up and coming market. The other concerned property in a London docklands development called Pan Peninsula ('Pan'). The latter in particular featured in the later months of 2007. Mr French had paid the first half of the deposit on the Pan property. A second instalment of the deposit was due on 1st November 2007.

18.   On or about 4th October 2007 the two men met at a restaurant called Tai Pan and discussed the nature of Mr Nisbet's indebtedness. Whether they reached an agreement and, if so, as to what amount Mr Nisbet owed was disputed.

19.   Mr French wanted to obtain an extension of the time within which he had to provide the second part of the deposit on the Pan development. In order to do this he wished to be able to show that he was due to receive monies shortly. He therefore urged Mr Nisbet to write him a comfort letter. At 7.53am on 9th October 2007 Mr French wrote

     'Its straightforward what ever your comfortable with ranging from 800k to 1.3 million the higher the better the more they think I have the more they will be prepared to wait do you I wouldnt ask but I know I am going to hit my deadlines and I need evidence to add the wait to may extension application thanks mate.'

20.   In response, Mr Nisbet wrote to Mr French on the same day

     'Further to our conversation earlier today, I am writing to confirm the position we are in and detail timescales for monies to be paid to our company and yourself in turn.

     With regard to the recent money you have lent me earlier this year, we will be in a position to pay the £123k back with interest at 20% per annum by 19th Nov '07.

     The Albany scheme has taken a lot longer to complete due to the problems encountered and I would anticipate this being finalised, bank paid etc by Jan/Feb '08. Depending on the level of success upon completion we would then be in a position to pay between £650k and £1m....'

21.   Mr French was dissatisfied with this version. He thought that the 'Albany scheme' should be changed to 'Albany Crown' and the amount in the final paragraph of my quotation should be changed to

'750k (the combined cost of my 2 mortgages as offered by you from your Albany apartments1.3 million deal) and 1.3 million the sum you agreed in the restaurant if money owed was not returned by November 1st and I was not able to back my London projects.'

22.   Mr Nisbet went some distance (but not all of the way) to meeting these requests. A second version of his letter did change the 'Albany scheme' to 'Albany Crown' and the final sentence of my quotation of the previous version was changed to 'We would then be in a position to pay £750k.' Mr Nisbet sent this version with a covering email which said

'I am not happy with this letter, in particular due to the content of what is in the book and my belief that there will be an investigation. A letter like this when they go into your finances, whilst I believe you are as clean as a whistle, will only drag me into the investigation, if not already, when I know I have done nothing wrong.'

23.   The 'Albany Crown' scheme referred to a plot of land which Crown owned in Manchester. There was existing planning permission for a number of serviced apartments. Mr Nisbet's preferred option, however, was to enter into a Joint Venture with a developer who could provide the finance for a bigger project that would have involved a large hotel as well as various other uses for the land. This would have needed new planning permission.

24.   From the middle of October 2007 Mr French began to suggest to Mr Nisbet that he should sell the Crown building. Mr French had a possible buyer in mind whom he understood would be willing to pay £15 million. When Mr Nisbet said that this would not cover his liabilities of over £14 million, Mr French said that he thought he would be able to have the offer increased to £17 million. Mr French said (and said repeatedly) that he considered that this would allow Mr Nisbet to meet his liabilities, pay what he owed to Mr French and still make a profit.

25.   The two men had been in regular email or text contact, but on 24th October 2007 Mr Nisbet emailed to say that 'I've lost a lot of time and focus over the last couple of weeks with all our discussions over what I'm doing.' Nonetheless, the communications continued from both of them.

26.   On 28th October 2007 Mr French sent Mr Nisbet a copy of a letter which he asked him to forward to the Liverpool police. This referred to two attempts to murder relatives of Mr French and to his fear that he himself would be the victim of a murder attempt.

27.   Meanwhile Mr Nisbet had continued his negotiations with potential Joint Venturers for the Crown site. By the end of October draft heads of agreement had been discussed with Harte Holdings and a rather more detailed draft heads of agreement with Byrne Estates, who would have been Mr Nisbet's first choice.

28.   On 31st October 2007 Mr French again pressed Mr Nisbet to take seriously the idea of selling the Crown site outright. He said that the current offer was £17 million, but he felt that it could be raised to £18 million. Mr Nisbet replied the same day. He said that he was disappointed that Mr French should question his friendship. He said also that the intermediary (Will Labella) who had been used by Mr French had stated that there had been no increase in the offered purchase price. However, Mr Nisbet did not appear to object in principle to the idea of selling the site. He said, 'As stated, if you can get £18m offer, then I would be more than happy to progress.' He concluded 'I cannot be working any harder to try and get a resolution on this and your assistance in getting an £18m would be most appreciated.'

29.   Mr Nisbet continued to explore with Mr Labella the possibility of a sale of the Crown site although there seem to have been complications because of assurances to Manchester City Council that the site would not be sold.

30.   Mr French had not been able to pay the second part of his deposit for the Pan project but he continued to seek an extension of time to do so. On 9th November 2007 Mr Nisbet wrote to Mr French. He apologised for not being able to repay the loans by 1st November On the same date he wrote a letter on behalf of Assets referring to a loan of £13,000 with interest at 20% p.a. The letter concluded 'As you are aware we shall shortly be concluding a joint venture agreement and we anticipate being in a position to reimburse you the outstanding amount within the next three months.'

31.   Two days later Mr French sent an email to Mr Nisbet setting out what he had understood Mr Nisbet had agreed was owing at the Tai Pan restaurant at the beginning of October. It totalled £1.3million. This was followed by a series of emails, phone messages and text messages from Mr French to Mr Nisbet, one theme of which was that it was ridiculous for Mr Nisbet to say that he felt threatened. On 13th November Mr Nisbet sent a text to say that he wished all further communication to be made via his solicitor. He said 'I would appreciate no further harassment to allow me to do my job which will enable me to realise cash to pay creditors including S&D'. JST wrote to Mr French in similar terms the same day.

32.   Mr French did continue to send texts, emails and phone messages over the following days.

33.   From about the middle of November, Mr Nisbet was also contacted by two other associates of Mr French, Marlon Campbell and Darren Alcock, who also encouraged him to sell the Crown site. They told him that they were to receive £250,000 each if the transaction went through. Mr Nisbet was puzzled as to why they should be due to receive such large sums. Darren Alcock was also known to have had a criminal conviction for attacking someone with a hot iron. The conviction had been many years previously. Although Mr Nisbet felt somewhat alarmed by the involvement of Alcock and Campbell, he agreed that they had never threatened him.

34.   There is a hiatus in Mr Nisbet's records of communications between 26th November and 15th December although his recollection was that the alleged harassment by Mr French did subside somewhat at the beginning of December.

35.   On 29th November 2007 Ms Summers wrote to Mr French. She set out the amounts which Mr Nisbet accepted he owed S&D (£118,850 plus interest), noted that 'Chris is at a crucial stage of negotiations with two potential joint venture partners with Albany Crown Ltd. They are time consuming and have required a fair amount of travel for Chris and his team.' She called on Mr French not to deflect Mr Nisbet from this work by his alternative proposals. She repeated that he did not wish to have any more communication with Mr French, but she was instructed to provide him with a weekly update if he did desist from direct contact.

36.   On 7th December 2007 Crown signed heads of agreement with Byrne Estates. According to an email from Heather Summers of that date 'there is now one preferred hotel operator with whom [Crown] will be immediately commencing negotiations'. I understand that that operator was one of the Virgin companies. By 14th December 2007 Mr Nisbet had managed to negotiate a release of some £25,000 from the bank. He arranged for £20,000 of this to be paid to S&D in part discharge of his debt.

37.   Mr French did manage to negotiate an extension of the time for him to make the second part of the deposit on the Pan project. The new deadline was 21st December 2007. As the time for this approached, Mr French again repeatedly expressed his anxiety that Mr Nisbet should pay the money that he thought was due to him. In his email of 15th December 2007 he ended by saying:

'You are very fortunate to find me at a point were I refuse to go backwards (the temptation to beat you to within an inch of your life i have rose above) I have turned my life around and money is no longer my be all and end all.'

38.   That email was sent a number of times over the next few days to Mr Nisbet and/or Ms Summers.

39.   Ms Summers wrote to Mr French on 19ᵗʰ December 2007. She objected to the barrage of emails as well as texts and calls. She threatened criminal or civil proceedings if the haranguing and undue pressure did not stop. While the debt (which is now the subject of S&D's claim) was acknowledged, she said that the larger sums claimed by Mr French were refuted.

40.   The 21ˢᵗ December 2007 deadline for Mr French to meet the second instalment of his deposit on the Pan project passed. He was not able to pay. As a result the first instalment was forfeited. That day he left a series of phone messages for Mr Nisbet. These did take on a threatening tone.

        At 12.20pm the message ended 'if you don't call me today, Chris, you personally, call me today and tell me that you're gonna cover my losses, I'm coming for you mate.'

        At 12.21pm (so immediately after the previous call), the message said 'The fact that you won't speak to me, the fact that your solicitor won't answer, the fact that I've been asking for an answer to this question for the last 21 days and you've totally ignored me, I've been absolutely livid, absolutely livid. In fact, I'm mad enough to go to prison. So you'd better call me and tell me that you're gonna cover my losses otherwise I'm really, really, gonna do something that we both regret.'

41.   At 2.07 he phoned and left a message apologising and promised that he would not harm Mr Nisbet. A yet further message was left for Ms Summers later that afternoon. He repeated his apology. After the message there was a long pause and, it seems, Mr French believed that the recording had stopped. It in fact continued and picked up what appears to have been Mr French talking to himself. He said:

        'I am just not going to let that guy drag me back down. He is trying to make me revert to …that I left behind and I do not want to do any more. Its just that I am absolutely outraged the lying twat. I should never have got involved with him I should have left him alone …(the Stephen of old?) would have blown his head off, but I am not that person anymore. I am against gun (violence and crime?) got to remember that got to try ??'

42.   In a final message at 4.0pm on 21ˢᵗ December, Mr French said

        'you nearly got me to revert to type, you nearly got me to come after ya in a physical way but I've managed to calm myself down and I've decided to let Pannones [the solicitors for S&D] deal with the bankruptcy.'

43.   Mr Nisbet said in evidence that he contacted the police on 21ˢᵗ December because of Mr French's behaviour.

44.   Later on 21ˢᵗ December 2007 Ms Summers emailed Mr French with an offer by Mr Nisbet. In summary, if it could be shown that the Pan project would have been profitable for Mr French, Mr Nisbet would reimburse him his lost deposit and his lost profit (Mr Nisbet had repeatedly made clear to Mr French that he thought that the Pan project was an unprofitable deal and, if anything, Mr French was fortunate that he had not been able to throw good money after bad by paying the second part of the deposit). This did not satisfy Mr French as he made clear in his email to her of 27ᵗʰ December 2007. He said that he intended to start bankruptcy proceedings.

S&D Property Investments v Nisbet

45.   Between 6th and 10th January 2008 Mr French left a series of phone messages for Mr Nisbet. These again had a threatening edge. Thus after calling round to Mr Nisbet's house on the afternoon of Sunday 6th January, he left a message at 4.33pm which concluded,

'That I can live with you dictating to me about what I can and can not do and losing me over 100k who do you think you are are you really that brave don't fuck with me any longer.'

46.   At 11.03am on 7th January 2008 his message began,

'Good morning send me the Friday up dates (something you yourself initiated) or I will come and get updated personally you may be brave in your own little world but when I stand before you what will you do so be a good little boy and do what you said you will do.'

47.   At 7.43pm on 10th January 2008 he said

'I need to see the back of you so do the right thing and stop fucking around. Let this be over.'

48.   On 11th January 2008 Ms Summers wrote what was effectively a letter before action threatening Mr French with an injunction under the Protection from Harassment Act if he did not stop contacting Mr Nisbet.

49.   It is not clear when Mr French received that letter. He denied that he had done so by the next day (12th January 2008) when he agrees that he attended Mr Nisbet's home. He says it was twice. Mr Nisbet and his girl-friend, Rebecca Davies Jones, say that it was three times. They allege that he behaved in a verbally aggressive and threatening manner. Ms Davies Jones in a statement made to the police shortly afterwards says that he said things such as, 'If you call the old bill I will set the boys on you'; 'Remember if I'm locked up, I have the perfect alibi'; 'Come out and face me like a man'; 'you think I'm harassing you now, let me tell you, it's not even begun'. It is not alleged that either of them was physically assaulted.

50.   Mr Nisbet called the police who came to the property. They spoke to Mr French. At 5.34pm that evening Mr French left a further phone message for Mr Nisbet which said,

'Hi Chris Stephen, just had a chat with the police n that. I'm on my way home now. Er like I explained to them, it's about evidence, If there's no evidence, there's no case. So it's as simple as I don't make threats. Never have done, never will do. I tried to speak to you amicably and friendly. You don't want to know, you wanna play silly buggers and now you are 100% my enemy. I don't like you any more brother. See you around.'

51.   About an hour later Mr French returned to Mr Nisbet's home and shouted more abuse. He left a series of further phone messages. His message at 6.30pm included the following,

'Listen I'm not one of your white business colleagues you know. I'm a nasty nigger. A real dirty, nasty street nigger. Do you understand?'

52.   On 14th January 2008 Mr French again went to Mr Nisbet's home in the morning as he and Ms Davies-Jones were about to leave the house in a car. He again shouted abuse at them. She says that as he left he pointed his hand towards Mr Nisbet in a gesture that imitated a gun. Again, it is not alleged that any physical assault took place.

S&D Property Investments v Nisbet

53.   Once again the police were called.

54.   Mr French was charged with threatening, abusive or insulting words or behaviour with intent to cause Mr
         Nisbet harassment, alarm or distress on 12th and 14th January 2008 contrary to s. 4A(1) and (5) of the Public
         Order Act 1986. He pleaded not guilty but, on 21st July 2008 he was convicted. He was conditionally discharged
         for 18 months and ordered to £200 prosecution costs. The Court refused to order compensation because,
         according to the memorandum of conviction, 'the complainant is indebted to the defendant by a very large
         amount, also the considerable provocation by the complainant.'

The Protection from Harassment Act 1997

55.   Section 1 of the Act prohibits harassment. It says:

         '(1) A person must not pursue a course of conduct –
                  (a)   which amounts to harassment of another, and
                  (b)   which he knows or ought to know amounts to harassment of the other.
         (2) For the purposes of this section, the person whose course of conduct is in question ought to know
         that it amounts to harassment of another if a reasonable person in possession of the same information
         would think the course of conduct amounted to harassment of the other....'

56.   By s.7

         '(2) References to harassing a person include alarming the person or causing the person distress.
         (3) A 'course of conduct' must involve conduct on at least two occasions.
         (4) 'Conduct' includes speech.'

57.   Section 2 of the Act makes harassment a summary offence. Section 3 creates a civil remedy for harassment. It
         says:

         '(1) An actual or apprehended breach of s.1 may be the subject of a claim in civil proceedings by the
         person who is or may be the victim of the course of conduct in question.
         (2) On such a claim, damages may be awarded for (among other things) any anxiety caused by the
         harassment and any financial loss resulting from the harassment...'

58.   A great deal of the vicissitudes of daily life might cause a person distress, but the courts have been clear that the
         conduct will not amount to harassment for the purposes of the 1997 Act unless it reaches a particular level. Thus
         in *Majrowski v Guy's and St Thomas's NHS Trust* [2007] 1 AC 224 Lord Nicholls said at [30]

         'Where ... the quality of the conduct said to constitute harassment is being examined, courts will
         have in mind that irritations, annoyances, even a measure of upset, arise at times in everybody's day-
         to-day dealings with other people. Courts are well able to recognise the boundary between conduct
         which is unattractive, even unreasonable, and conduct which is oppressive and unacceptable. To
         cross the boundary from the regrettable to the unacceptable the gravity of the misconduct must be of
         an order which would sustain criminal liability under s.2.'

59.   Baroness Hale said at [66]

         'A great deal is left to the wisdom of the courts to draw sensible lines between the ordinary banter
         and badinage of life and genuinely offensive and unacceptable behaviour.'

S&D Property Investments v Nisbet

60.   In *Conn v Sunderland City Council* [2008] IRLR 324 at [12] Gage LJ said:

'It seems to me that what, in the words of Lord Nicholls in Majrowski, crosses the boundary between unattractive and even unreasonable conduct and conduct which is oppressive and unacceptable, may well depend on the context in which the conduct occurs. What might not be harassment on the factory floor or in the barrack room might well be harassment in the hospital ward and vice versa. In my judgment the touchstone for recognizing what is not harassment for the purposes of sections 1 and 3 will be whether the conduct is of such gravity as to justify the sanctions of the criminal law.'

61.   In *Ferguson v British Gas Trading* [2009] EWCA Civ 46 Jacob LJ said:

'17. I accept that a course of conduct must be grave before the offence or tort of harassment is proved. And that, as Mr Porter accepted after some discussion, the only real difference between the crime of s.2 and the tort of s.3 is standard of proof. To prove the civil wrong of harassment it is necessary to prove the case on a balance of probabilities, to prove the crime, the standard is the usual criminal one of beyond a reasonable doubt.

18. In so accepting I would just add this word of caution: the fact of parallel criminal and civil liability is not generally, outside the particular context of harassment, of significance in considering civil liability. There are a number of other civil wrongs which are also crimes. Perhaps most common would be breaches of the Trade Descriptions Act 1968 as amended. In the field of intellectual property both trade mark and copyright infringement, and the common law tort of passing off (which generally involves deception), may all amount to crimes. It has never been suggested generally that the scope of a civil wrong is restricted because it is also a crime. What makes the wrong of harassment different and special is because, as Lord Nicholls and Lady Hale recognised, in life one has to put up with a certain amount of annoyance: things have got to be fairly severe before the law, civil or criminal, will intervene.'

Was any part of what Mr French did a course of conduct amounting to harassment and, if so, which part?

62.   In my judgment until 15ᵗʰ December 2007 Mr French's behaviour did not cross the threshold of gravity necessary to amount to harassment. Mr Nisbet acknowledged his indebtedness to S&D at least to the sum of some £113,000 plus interest. Mr Nisbet recognised that repayment of this sum was overdue and that the failure to repay it was causing acute difficulties for Mr French himself and/or his company. There was or may have been a disagreement as to whether Mr Nisbet owed the very much larger sums which Mr French claimed. These were essentially business disputes and, as Gage LJ. said, the context in which the acts occur is important in determining whether they amount to harassment.

63.   Mr French's communications were frequent at times. He was persistent in expressing his strongly held view that Mr Nisbet would be better off in selling the Crown site. He was sometimes repetitious. Mr Nisbet and JST Lawyers both wrote to Mr French on 13ᵗʰ November 2007 saying that all further communications should go via the solicitor. The volume of communications from Mr French to Mr Nisbet direct declined. The fact that they did not cease is matter for me to take into account, but is not, in my view, determinative.

64.   I am not persuaded that Mr Nisbet was afraid of Mr French at this stage. Mr French had had a reputation for extreme violence, but that was long in the past. I think that the remark about Mr Moule and Mr Mason probably was an off-hand and was immediately retracted. In any case, though, Mr Nisbet later renewed his friendship and business dealings with Mr French despite this incident. There were no threats from Mr French during this period. Mr French was an international kick boxing champion, but I do not consider that this takes the matter much further. Mr French explained that it was essentially a form of self defence. There is no evidence that he used his skill offensively. The flow of consciousness style which Mr French adopted in his emails, texts and phone messages makes it somewhat easier to perceive his intentions. On the basis of them and his evidence, I do not regard them as intimidatory. Mr Nisbet said that he was frightened by the death threats against Mr French and his relatives, but I found it difficult to understand how these matters, which were (apparently) aimed at Mr French should have led Mr Nisbet to fear Mr French. Neither Mr Alcock nor Mr Campbell threatened Mr Nisbet. Mr Nisbet said that he felt pressured by Mr French into writing his comfort letters of 9ᵗʰ October and 9ᵗʰ November 2007, yet it is striking that neither complied entirely with Mr French's wishes. Finally, I note that Mr

S&D Property Investments v Nisbet

Nisbet did not at this stage go to the police. This contrasts with his reaction to Mr French's behaviour in on 21st December.

65. In my view the position changed with the series of emails beginning on 15th December 2007 in which Mr French referred to the temptation to beat Mr Nisbet within an inch of his life. Even though Mr French said that he had risen above that temptation, the express allusion by Mr French to his violent past crossed the boundary. It was no longer merely unattractive and unreasonable but became oppressive and unacceptable. I am strengthened in this view because Mr French sent this same email on a number of occasions.

66. I have said above that Mr French's telephone messages on 21st December 2007 took on a threatening tone. These came only two days after Heather Summers' email of 19th December 2007 which had called on him to stop haranguing her client. I find that the telephone messages which he left on 21st December were further acts of harassment.

67. The text messages which Mr French sent to Mr Nisbet at 4.33 on 6th January 2008, 11.03am on 7th January and 7.43 on 10th January were likewise oppressive and unacceptable and amounted to further harassment.

68. Mr French's visits to Mr Nisbet's home on 12th January and 14th January were the subject of the criminal conviction. I have set out above the particulars of the charge under the Public Order Act 1986 which he faced. While he was not prosecuted under the Protection from Harassment Act 1997, the acts which he was proved to have done on that day plainly amounted to harassment within the meaning of that Act.

69. Criminal and civil liability under the 1997 Act arises only if the person concerned 'knows or ought to know [that his course of conduct] amounts to harassment of the other.'

70. Whether or not Mr French did know that his conduct amounted to harassment, I find that he ought to have done so. He was put on notice by the email from Heather Summers of 19th December 2007 that his letters of the previous few days had been regarded as haranguing, undue pressure and an implied threat and, if they did not cease, would lead to action in the criminal or civil courts. In any case, and even without that letter, it would have been apparent to any reasonable person that the messages of 21st December and those between 6th and 10th January 2008 which I have mentioned above would amount to harassment. The criminal conviction was dependent on proof that Mr French intended to cause Mr Nisbet harassment alarm or distress on 12th and 14th January.

71. Civil liability under the 1997 Act only arises if there was a course of conduct which involves conduct on at least two occasions. That condition is plainly satisfied here.

Damages for Anxiety

72. Section 3(2) of the 1997 Act says that damages can be awarded for 'anxiety' amongst other things. In my judgment, Parliament was here intending to make plain that compensation could be given for the concern that harassment can generate even if it does not give rise to any psychiatric or medical condition. Psychiatric harm is a well recognised form of personal injury. Where a statute creates civil liability it would not be usual for Parliament to specify the particular types of physical harm or personal injury which are compensatable. It would go without saying that psychiatric harm (if proved and if satisfying the other usual conditions such as causation and forseeability) would be recoverable. The express reference to 'anxiety' must be intended to convey something more. In any case, it would be inapt to use this term if it was intended to be limited to a mental state that was so severe as to amount to an illness.

73. Ms Dainty on behalf of Mr French and S&D appeared to accept that 'anxiety' short of psychiatric harm could be the subject of compensation. However, she submitted in her written argument that even in such cases there ought to be medical evidence. Otherwise, she argued, the court would not be able to distinguish a groundless from a well-founded claim for damages.

74. I am not sure that she persisted in that position in oral argument. However, in any case, I do not agree with it. If, as I hold, 'anxiety' is not limited to conditions which amount to psychiatric harm, medical evidence cannot be the exclusive means of proving the loss. *Martins v Choudhary* [2007] EWCA Civ 1379 does not help. Medical evidence had been available in that discrimination case. But the Claimant was there seeking (and was awarded) damages for both psychiatric harm and injury to feelings. That is not the situation in the present case. Evidence of anxiety can instead come from lay witnesses: the victim of the harassment and those around him or her. The court can also take into account what is likely to have been the effect of the harassment in question.

75. In *Majrowski* at [29] Lord Nicholls said that damages for anxiety under the 1997 Act would 'normally be modest'. It is not entirely clear whether this was a matter of competing argument on the appeal. The issue in that case was whether an employer could be vicariously liable for harassment by one of its employees. Lord Nicholls was dealing with the defendant's floodgates argument. The defendant was arguing that there would be significant difficulties for the employer in dealing with such claims even if damages for anxiety in an individual case were not large. Neither side, it seems, was arguing that damages under the Act would be other than 'modest'.

76. Whatever the status of Lord Nicholls' remark I respectfully suggest that as a prediction it is likely to be correct. If one sets aside cases where psychiatric damage has occurred, the approach of the courts in other areas where compensation can be awarded for anxiety and distress, shows that damages are not likely to be particularly high. In *Vento v Chief Constable of West Yorkshire (No.2)* [2003] ICR 318 the Court of Appeal gave guidance as to the level of damages for injury to feelings caused by discrimination. It said:

> '(i) The top band should normally be between £15,000 and £25,000. Sums in this range should be awarded in the most serious cases, such as where there has been a lengthy campaign of discriminatory harassment on the ground of sex or race. This case falls within that band. Only in the most exceptional case should an award of compensation for injury to feelings exceed £25,000.
>
> (ii) The middle band between £5,000 and £15,000 should be used for serious cases, which do not merit an award in the highest band.
>
> (iiii) Awards of between £500 and £5,000 are appropriate for less serious cases, such as where an act of discrimination is an isolated or one off occurrence. In general, awards of less than £500 are to be avoided altogether, as they risk being regarded as so low as not to be a proper recognition of injury to feelings.'

77. I accept Ms Dainty's submission that it would be wrong simply to apply the same bands to harassment cases. Compensation for discrimination necessarily involves an award for the humiliation of being treated differently on an impermissible ground such as race or sex. That is not a necessary feature of a claim under the 1997 Act. On the other hand, it is an essential characteristic of a claim under that Act that there has been a course of conduct. There will not be a case where damages for harassment have to be assessed for an isolated or one off occurrence.

78. In the present case, Mr Nisbet gave evidence that Mr French's behaviour had had a severe impact on him. He had slept poorly. He attended his office infrequently. He had not been able to concentrate. He had been very afraid. He felt oppressed by Mr French's repeated demands and had done what he could to avoid antagonising him further. He said he had hardly been able to produce any meaningful work. Ms Davies Jones gave evidence that he had not been working in the evenings as he usually did and that he was sleeping poorly. Mr Douglas, Mr Nisbet's business partner also gave evidence that he had been distracted by Mr French's activities.

79.   I have concluded that I need to approach this evidence with considerable caution for a number of reasons. The actions of Mr French which I have found to amount to harassment are far fewer and over a much shorter time span that Mr Nisbet alleged. In particular, up to 15ᵗʰ December 2007 I have found that the communications from Mr French did not cross the boundary into the oppressive and unacceptable. It may well have been distracting and stressful for Mr Nisbet to deal with them. The fact remains, however, that on his own case, he owed Mr French well over £100,000. He knew that Mr French was particularly anxious to be paid because he himself was committed to making a second payment on the Pan project and risked losing the first payment in default. Mr Nisbet's inability to make this payment was symptomatic of his own precarious financial position. It would not be at all surprising if these money problems caused Mr Nisbet to be distracted and to sleep poorly.

80.   Furthermore, I cannot find on the balance of probabilities that Mr French engendered fear in Mr Nisbet until (at the earliest) the actions which I have found to constitute harassment. Mr French's violent past was behind him when he first met Mr Nisbet in 1996. There is no evidence that Mr French has engaged in any actual violence since then. Mr Nisbet referred to Mr French's threat to his co-directors in April 2005, but that was followed swiftly by an apology on Mr French's behalf. Nothing actually occurred. Even if his remarks at the meeting in June 2005 support the case that the remarks had been made, what Mr French was doing was emphasising the withdrawal rather than renewing the threat. More importantly, Mr Nisbet continued to deal with Mr French despite that remark. And in January 2007, their business and friendly relationship revived. In March - September 2007, Mr French provided Mr Nisbet with much-needed financial support.

81.   Nor was I persuaded that the events of September - mid-December 2007 were such as to generate a fear of Mr French in Mr Nisbet. Mr Nisbet did instruct his solicitors to write to Mr French on 19ᵗʰ December 2007 threatening criminal and civil proceedings. He contacted the police on 21ˢᵗ December and again on the occasions when Mr French came to his house. Had Mr Nisbet really been afraid of Mr French earlier in the sequence of events, I see no reason why he would not at that stage have gone to police or threatened proceedings.

82.   That leaves a period of about a month during which I have found that there was a course of conduct amounting to harassment. I have accepted that there was a threatening tone to the messages on 21ˢᵗ December and the ones in early January. I accept that those engendered feelings of anxiety in Mr Nisbet. So, too, must the repeated visits of Mr French to Mr Nisbet's house. I accept that the contemporary accounts of Mr Nisbet and Ms Davies-Jones give an accurate flavour of the kind of remarks which Mr French made on those occasions. The anxiety and distress which Mr Nisbet must have felt on those occasions would have been prompted in part because of fears for his own safety and in part because of his concern for Ms Davies Jones. I see no reason why damages for this harassment which was targeted at him should not reflect both elements of his anxiety and distress.

83.   So far as foreseeability is a necessary element of a claim for damages under the 1997 Act, it is satisfied. I have found that the course of conduct pursued by Mr French was one which he either knew or ought to have known would cause alarm or distress.

84.   Overall I consider that the right sum to compensate Mr Nisbet for the anxiety which I have found is £7,000.

85.   There was some evidence as to an incident in the Wallasey Tunnel in October 2008. Both Mr French and Mr Nisbet were driving through the Tunnel. It is alleged that Mr French drove in an intimidating manner. Mr French disputed this. It is unnecessary for me to make a finding as to this. It was not pleaded as part of the harassment for which Mr Nisbet was entitled to compensation. The course of conduct pleaded in Mr Nisbet's defence and counterclaim ran from October 2007 to January 2008 (see paragraph 7). Ms Davies-Jones also alleged that later in 2008 Mr French had behaved in a threatening manner to her at a gym which they both attended. Again this was disputed. Again I need make no findings. Ms Davies-Jones is not a party to the action. Mr Nisbet has not sought to plead this incident.

Damages for financial loss?

86.   Mr Nisbet alleges that because of Mr French's harassment he was unable to give his full and proper attention to his companies' business. He claims that he alone was able to negotiate with the potential joint venture partners and hoteliers. Although Heads of Terms were negotiated with two joint venture partners, the harassment meant that he was unable to devote time to the necessary follow-through. In particular, he alleges that he missed a series of weekly internal development meetings on 11th and 25th October; 8th and 22nd November; 6th, 13th and 20th December and 10th and 24th January 2008.

87.   Mr Nisbet's further says that in consequence of Crown and Assets losing valuable business, he, as the sole shareholder also suffered loss.

88.   Ms Dainty submitted: (a) It had not been shown on the balance of probabilities that any of Mr Nisbet's companies had failed to secure either a joint venture contract or a hotel contract or suffered delay as a result of any harassment; (b) there was no scope for the 'loss of a chance' principle; (c) in any case, any such loss was not reasonably foreseeable and for that reason was not recoverable; (d) further, this head of loss (if otherwise proved) was reflective of the loss suffered by the companies. As such, Mr Nisbet could not claim it consistently with the principle in cases such as *Johnson v Gore Wood* [2001] 1 All ER 481.

89.   It will be recalled that because of the order of HHJ Stephen Davies I must determine whether or not Mr French's harassment caused any delay in the Manchester project and whether or not there is liability for any such delay. If I answered those questions favourably to Mr Nisbet, quantification of loss would be dealt with at a further hearing.

Causation

90.   At this stage, I apply the 'but for' test of causation i.e. whether on the balance of probabilities Mr Nisbet has shown that, but for Mr French's harassment, Crown or Assets would have secured a joint venture agreement and/or an agreement with a hotelier and/or would have made either contract at an earlier stage. At one stage Mr Horne, on behalf of Mr Nisbet, argued that it would be sufficient if the harassment materially contributed to the financial loss. However, he did not pursue that argument at the hearing.

91.   In my judgment, Mr Nisbet has not satisfied the 'but for' test.

92.   I consider first the allegation that the harassment caused Mr Nisbet to miss the specified weekly internal meetings.

93.   I note first that only three of these (20th December, 10th January and 24th January) took place after the course of conduct which I have found to constitute harassment began. If indeed Mr Nisbet had missed 6 other internal weekly meetings before then, I cannot be sure that any difficulties he encountered was because of him missing the last three rather than the earlier meetings.

94.   Secondly, it emerged in the course of Mr Nisbet's evidence that he may have missed at least some of the meetings because of other reasons. He said that the harassment lessened in the early part of December. He said specifically that the meetings that had been due to take place on 6th, 13th and 20th December may have been cancelled for other reasons. The last of these was one of only three internal meetings which had taken place after what I have found to be Mr French's course of harassment commenced.

95.   The next internal meeting was due to take place on 10th January 2008. In a letter from Mr Nisbet's solicitor of 11th January 2008 to Mr French she said:

> 'As a result of this lost time, Chris had to cancel an important meeting in London scheduled for 10 January with the Joint Venture partner and hotelier and instead had to conduct this meeting by way of telephone conference.'

96.   It must be open to doubt whether an internal meeting could have been held in Liverpool (where the head office of Crown and Assets was located and the internal meetings took place) on the same day as such a meeting in London, but even if it could, it is difficult to see why that meeting (like the one that was due to take place in London) could not also have been conducted by way of a telephone conference instead.

97.   Thirdly, the significance of Mr Nisbet missing these meetings was unclear to say the least. Five of them had or should have taken place before 7th December 2007 when the heads of agreement with Byrne Estates were signed. Mr Nisbet's witness statement of 21st January 2008 said that before Christmas 2007 excellent progress had been made with both the joint venture and the hotel scheme. In his oral evidence he accepted that the prospects for the joint venture were still good despite his absences from the internal meetings. In his email to Mr French of 31st October 2007 Mr Nisbet said 'I cannot be working any harder.' The email traffic showing Mr Nisbet's personal involvement with the negotiations with Byrne Estates and Harte Holdings at about this time supports this comment. I did not accept his oral evidence in which he said that that statement was incorrect.

98.   Fourthly, it was entirely unclear what was due to take place at these meetings. Mr Nisbet said in evidence that a bullet point list of issues to be discussed was produced, but none of these lists had been disclosed. Other than in the most general terms, Mr Nisbet could not assist in what had been on the agendas for these meetings. Nor was it clear why the meetings could not have been rearranged rather than cancelled.

99.   Overall, I consider that the evidence about the internal meetings provided very little assistance for Mr Nisbet on the causation issue.

100.   Mr Nisbet also produced a survey of emails sent from his office during the period June 2007 – December 2008. In October 2007 there had been 484. In July – December 2008 there had also been over 400 each month. By contrast in November 2007 there had been none. In December 76. There had been no more 6 each month from January – April 2008 and 13 in June 2008. The survey comments 'All other emails were sent via laptop on separate Outlook account, which proves I was out of the office and house working off a data card.'

101.   It is not quite clear what Mr Nisbet meant by 'separate Outlook account'. The trial bundle includes several emails sent during November 2007 from the address chris.nisbet@albanyassets.com, which Mr Nisbet said, was his only business email account. So during the month when his survey recorded no emails sent from his office, he was far from inactive. I recall as well that despite the lack of emails sent from his office in November, the heads of agreement were signed with Byrne Estates in early December and 'excellent progress' was also made with the hotelier.

102.   Apart from the meetings, the Schedule of Loss is wholly imprecise as to the causal links between the harassment and its impact on the Crown project. Paragraph 6, for instance, says

> 'A number of tasks were also delayed due to the ongoing harassment. These were tasks throughout October, November and December which delayed matters by 3 – 4 months and lead to certain offers

being withdrawn. Heads of terms were agreed in respect of a couple of joint venture partners which as a result of [Mr Nisbet] being unable to dedicate his full and proper attention to the business these deals did not proceed.'

103.   In his witness statement of 1st April 2009 paragraphs 8 & 9 Mr Nisbet said:

'The second joint venture partner who could have been progressed was Byrne Estates...However, due to the intervening harassment by Mr French as set out in my earlier witness statement nothing was progressed in relation to the joint venture partners, the hotel agreement on indeed anything particularly on this site from about September/October 2007 through to February / March 2008.'

104.   This comment is not accurate. Mr Nisbet confirmed in his evidence that the heads of agreement with Byrne had been signed on 7th December. It is also inconsistent with paragraph 26 of his first witness statement in which he had said that before Christmas 2007 'excellent progress [had been] made with both the JV and the hotel' and, as a result the bank had released £25,000.

105.   The evidence as to the period over which Mr French's harassment was alleged to have impacted on Mr Nisbet was also inconsistent. Mr Nisbet's witness statement of 1st April 2009 said that he had been unable to work between October 2007 and January 2008 (paragraph 10) or February 2008 (paragraph 24). In cross examination, however, he said that it was only in July 2008 that he went back to work full time. This change appears to have been prompted by the email survey which, as I have already mentioned, appeared to show a substantial diminution in emails being sent from Mr Nisbet's office between November 2007 and June 2008. However, if Mr Nisbet's performance had been affected until July 2008, I find it remarkable that not only he but also Ms Davies Jones and Mr Douglas in their witness statements of 1st April 2009 should have spoken of the impact lasting only until February 2008. This reinforces my scepticism as to the usefulness of the email survey. It also, I am afraid, underlines my concern as to Mr Nisbet's tendency to exaggerate. In his oral evidence, Mr Douglas said that the impact of the harassment had continued through to March or July 2008. The inconsistency between this and his witness statement made me doubt the reliance which I could place on his evidence.

106.   There were two other parts of Mr Nisbet's evidence which have led me to be cautious in accepting his evidence.

107.   The first was a passage at the beginning of his first witness statement where he said 'My background and qualifications are as a Quantity Surveyor.' In cross examination he said that he had spent three years studying quantity surveying, but he then left to go into business. He did not complete the degree or have any other qualifications in quantity surveying.

108.   The second was his explanation as to why he did not go to see his General Practitioner when (on his account) his anxiety about Mr French's harassment was preventing him from sleeping and working. He said that he did not want to explain to the GP that Mr French had threatened his life because he wanted to be able to look to the GP to provide a medical report in support of an application for life insurance. He feared that he would not be offered life insurance if the GP included in the report a reference to his belief that his life had been threatened. There are two alternative conclusions to be drawn from this. One is that he positively wished to conceal from the life insurer information which he knew to be relevant. The other is that he did not really believe his life was under threat. Neither reflects well on Mr Nisbet's credibility.

109.   Mr Nisbet's witness statement of 1st April 2009 produced copy emails of 18th October 2007 and 23rd October 2007 which he said showed that heads of terms had actually been agreed. I have mentioned above that in his oral evidence, Mr Nisbet said that Heads of Terms with Byrne Estates were finally agreed on 7th December 2007. A copy of those final terms was not produced in evidence. I do not know to what extent they differed from the attachment to Mr Nisbet's email of 23rd October, but at several points that document alludes to the need for further details. This document aside, there is no evidence at all from Byrne Estates, nor from their agent, Grant Thornton. In the course of his evidence, Mr Nisbet said that Byrne never exchanged contracts and in March or

April 2008, they pulled away. It is a curious (an unsatisfactory) feature of Mr Nisbet's April 2009 witness statement that it said nothing about these developments let alone why they happened. I certainly have no independent evidence as to why this was, whether it had anything to do with Mr Nisbet being distracted by Mr French's activities or whether there was some other reason. The 23rd October 2007 draft contemplates that various conditions had to be fulfilled before exchange of contracts would take place. I do not know whether exchange failed to take place because one of these conditions (or some other condition) was not fulfilled and, if that was the case, why the condition was not fulfilled.

110.   Ms Dainty is also entitled to make the point that at least three of Mr Nisbet's companies (Crymark, Albany Building and Albany Irwell) either went into liquidation or receivership.

111.   Overall I am very far from being persuaded on a balance of probabilities that, but for the course of conduct which I have found Mr French committed, Mr Nisbet's companies would have secured a joint venture contract or would have done so sooner.

112.   The evidence as to the development of relations with hoteliers was even thinner. In the autumn of 2007 there were negotiations with Virgin. I have very little information about their progress. I have mentioned above Mr Nisbet's witness statement which said that excellent progress had been made with the hotelier (as well as the JV) by Christmas 2007. I also note that in the course of the trial an email was produced from Heather Summers dated 22nd March 2008. It said that heads (I assume of agreement) had been signed with a hotelier. Mr Douglas said that this was with Virgin.

113.   Once again I am unable to find that delay (if there was any) in reaching agreement with a hotelier was due to the harassment by Mr French.

Loss of a chance

114.   Normally a claimant must prove that but for the defendant's wrongdoing he would have gained the advantage for which he seeks compensation. This is compatible with the underlying purpose of damages in tort which is to put the claimant in as good a position as if the tort had not been committed.

115.   The 'loss of a chance' doctrine modifies the 'but for' test where the advantage in question depends on the hypothetical action of a third party. If there was a substantial chance that the third party would have acted so as to confer the benefit then the claimant is entitled to a percentage of the benefit to reflect what the Court judges to be the chance that the third party would have so conferred it – see for instance *Allied Maples Group Ltd v Simmons and Simmons* [1995] 1 WLR 1602 CA. Mr Horne invokes that principle in the present case.

116.   Ms Dainty submitted that the wording of s.3(2) of the Protection from Harassment Act 1997 ('financial loss resulting from the harassment') excluded the operation of the loss of a chance principle. I do not accept that argument. One way of viewing the principle is as a means of quantifying loss which results from a wrong in particular circumstances. On that basis, the language of the Act does not preclude the principle's operation.

117.   Nonetheless, in my judgment, there are several reasons why the 'loss of a chance' principle does not help Mr Nisbet.

(a)   Where the tort takes the form of a positive act, the Claimant must prove on the ordinary balance of probabilities what its impact was on him as a matter of historical fact - see *Allied*

S&D Property Investments v Nisbet

Maples above at p. 1609. Here I have accepted that Mr Nisbet was caused anxiety by the conduct of Mr French which constituted harassment – between 15th December 2007 and 14th January 2008 but I am not persuaded that this conduct led Mr Nisbet to be disabled from working during that period. At most I consider that it constituted a distraction.

(b) Even in cases where the Claimant can rely on 'loss of a chance' he must prove on the balance of probabilities that he would have been able and willing to have done what was necessary on his part to achieve the benefit but for the tort. Thus, for instance, where a claimant alleges that his solicitor's negligence has led to the loss of a chance of successfully litigating against a third party, the claimant must be ready to prove that (if properly represented) he would have pursued the claim. If he lacked the financial means to litigate in any event, the 'loss of a chance' principle has no part to play. I have already indicated that the heads of agreement with Byrne Estates is not in evidence. I know little about what further conditions had to be fulfilled for them to be translated into exchanged contracts. Mr Douglas said in evidence that it was necessary for a valuation to be prepared, but that was something which they would have commissioned others to perform. The valuation would not have been by Assets or Crown in house. It was unclear to me why this commission could not have been initiated by Mr Douglas. Absent the final heads of agreement, I could not tell whether there were other conditions that needed to be completed before exchange with Byrne Estates took place. Correspondingly, Mr Nisbet has not proved that, in the absence of Mr French's harassment, he (and Crown and Assets) had or would have been able to complete all the conditions which were their responsibility.

(c) Thirdly, there is the dearth of evidence as to why Byrne Estates pulled out. This means that Mr Nisbet cannot prove that this step was due to his inactivity brought about by Mr French's harassment. In any case, it also has the consequence that I simply lack any evidential basis on which I could assess the chance that such a contract would have been achieved in the absence of harassment.

Reasonable foreseeability and reflective loss

118. Because I consider that Mr Nisbet has failed to prove the necessary causal links between Mr French's harassment and any financial loss, the further issue of foreseeability of financial loss does not arise. Nor need I resolve the difficult issue of whether Mr Nisbet would anyway be debarred by the principle of reflective loss.

Vicarious liability of S&D for the harassment of Mr French

119. The House of Lords held in *Majrowski* that an employer could be vicariously liable for the harassment of its employee. It was not disputed in the present case that S&D could be vicariously liable for the harassment of Mr French if he acted as the company's agent and within the scope of his authority.

120. Mr French is and was a director of S&D. The other director was his wife Dionne French. In her witness statement of 8th April 2009 she said

'I am able to confirm that Stephen French, my husband, was not authorised by S&D to try and recover monies owed by Nisbet to S&D. Any actions that he took were on his own account and had absolutely nothing to do with S&D. In fact, if I had been aware of what it is alleged Stephen had done I would have taken steps to stop him from continuing to act in that manner.'

121. However, in her oral evidence she said that she was aware that money had been lent to Mr Nisbet. She knew that its repayment was needed in order to meet the second instalment of the deposit on the Pan project. Critically, she accepted that she left everything to do with the recovery of the debt to Stephen, 'Getting the money back was a matter for Stephen.'

122. I have no hesitation in accepting that her oral evidence is the more likely to be true. I conclude that Mr French was the agent of S&D for the purpose of taking steps to recover the debt. Plainly, it was left to his judgment as

to how this should be done. His harassment of Mr Nisbet was part and parcel of his attempts to do just that. Accordingly, I find that his harassment was within the scope of his actual authority. S& D is vicariously liable for his tort.

Set off

123.   A cross claim may constitute an equitable set off if it flows out of, and is inseparably connected with, the dealings or transactions which give rise to the subject of the claim and if it would be manifestly unjust to allow one to be enforced without regard to the other – see *Bim Kemi AB v Blackburn Chemicals Ltd* [2001] 2 Ll.Rep. 93 CA.

124.   In this case the harassment did flow out of Mr French's attempts to recover the debt which is the subject matter of the claim. There is an obvious and inseparable connection between the subject matters of the claim and counter claim. In my judgment it is also obvious that it would be manifestly unfair to allow S&D to enforce the full amount of its judgment debt without giving allowance for the damages that I have determined they must pay for Mr French's harassment.

125.   It was somewhat faintly argued by Ms Dainty that Mr Nisbet should not be allowed to rely on equitable set off since he did not come to court with 'clean hands'. It was submitted that his outstanding debt disentitled him to invoke equity. I reject this argument. The failure to pay a debt owed in law does not debar a litigant from relying on equitable principles.

126.   I will hear submissions as to how precisely my award affects the balance of debt owed by Mr Nisbet. My preliminary views, subject to those submissions, are that, the principal sum of the debt will be reduced by £7,000 as of 14th January 2008 and the interest due to S&D must also be reduced accordingly. The damages will also carry interest pursuant to s.35A of the Supreme Court Act 1981. Again, I will be grateful for submissions as to how this should be quantified.

Further proceedings and stay

127.   Because of the decisions to which I have come, there will be no need for expert evidence and (apart from the matters to which I have alluded in the previous section) no need for any further proceedings after this judgment has been handed down. Once judgment has been handed down, I propose to lift the stay on the enforcement of the balance of the debt owed by Mr Nisbet.

Summary of conclusions

128.   In summary, therefore, I conclude as follows:

a)   Mr French did engage in a course of conduct which amounted to harassment. That ran from 15th December 2007 – 14th January 2008.

b)   The harassment caused Mr Nisbet anxiety and distress.

c)   I award Mr Nisbet £7,000 in damages against Mr French.

d)   S&D Property Investment Ltd. authorised Mr French to take action to collect the debt due from Mr Nisbet. The harassment was within the scope of this authority. S&D is vicariously liable for it and is therefore also liable to pay Mr Nisbet £7,000 in damages.

e)   Mr Nisbet has not proved on the balance of probabilities that any financial loss resulted from the harassment. He is not assisted by the loss of a chance principle.

f)   The damages awarded to Mr Nisbet can be set off against the judgment sum already awarded to S&D. There will need to be further adjustments for interest.

g)   There is no need for any further hearing (save for finalising the consequences of this judgment). Mr Nisbet's application to call expert evidence is refused.

h)   The stay on enforcement of the judgment in S&D's favour will be lifted.

Index